S0-CWR-685

About This Book

Proceeds from this book will be donated to the United Way of the Quad Cities Area, Inc. The United Way is a vital part of the Quad Cities and surrounding communities, and proceeds from this book will assist in funding programs that help local families in need. Last year one in three area families were helped by the United Way of the Quad Cities Area, Inc.

Our special thanks go to Quad City Bank & Trust for their generous donation of financial assistance in order processing.

Contents

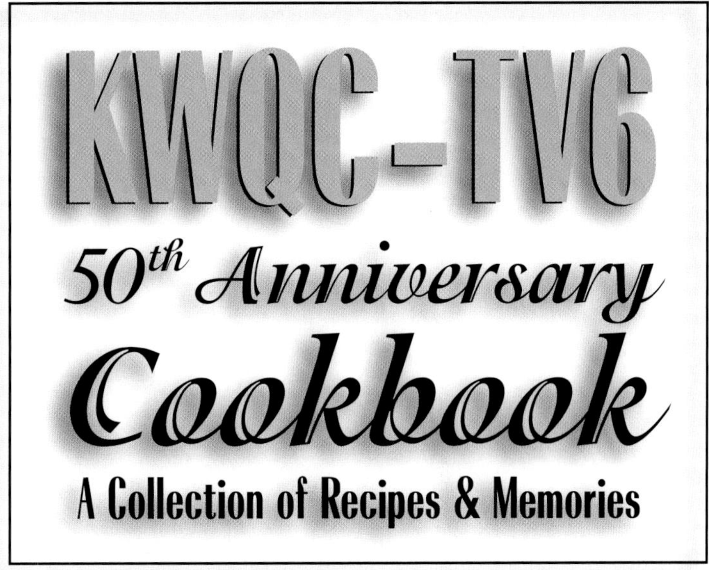

Celebrating A Half Century In Broadcasting

Paul Yeager

KWQC-TV6 50th Anniversary in Broadcasting,
a Collection of Recipes and Memories,
is dedicated to our loyal viewers
who have watched our station through the years.

This cookbook is a collection of favorite recipes,
which are not necessarily original recipes.

KWQC-TV6
805 Brady Street
Davenport, Iowa 52803
(319) 383-7000

Library of Congress Number: 98-075159
ISBN: 0-9666026-0-9

Designed, Edited, and Manufactured by
Favorite Recipes® Press
an imprint of

FRP™

P.O. Box 305142
Nashville, Tennessee 37230
1-800-358-0560

Book Design: Robin Crosslin
Project Manager: Judy Jackson
Art Director: Steve Newman

Manufactured in the United States of America
First Printing: 1998 15,000 copies

Photograph on page 83 courtesy of *Quad City Times*
Photograph on page 96 courtesy of Davenport Public Library Special Collections

Preface

Through the years we have had the honor of being involved in hundreds of community events that have benefitted different organizations. It is through the strength of our community that these events have succeeded. The goal of this book is to share some of the history of our station and some of the community events that have come to mean so much to the Quad Cities and surrounding communities.

Introduction

Jim Graham
Vice President and General Manager, KWQC-TV6

Through the years the success of KWQC-TV6 can be attributed to the loyalty of our viewers. Beginning on October 31, 1949, when WOC signed on the air, up to today, we have experienced the loyalty of thousands of viewers.

The philosophy of our station since the beginning has been to provide quality local programming, the best news programming in the market, and a strong presence and commitment to our communities and viewers.

During the past 50 years our viewers have enjoyed a wide variety of local programming, including "Trip the Trio," "Musical Moods," "Circus 6 Ranch," "Especially for You," "Five PM Live," and "Paula Sands Live." All these programs have involved the talents of many people, both in front of and behind the camera, and their commitment to quality is what has really made a difference in these programs.

We have also strived to provide the best news coverage for the Quad Cities and surrounding communities. We have documented many changes in the area, and we have always worked to keep our viewers informed. We have been honored through the years to have had some of the most dedicated and professional journalists in the news business. We have bid a fond farewell to many employees in our news department when they have had the opportunity to move on to larger markets such as Chicago, Denver, Minneapolis, Orlando, and St. Louis, but it was with a sense of pride and accomplishment that we watched them go.

Our greatest strength and pride as a station has been our involvement in and with the community. Our responsibility for the past 50 years has been to serve the needs of our viewers, and we feel that our ongoing responsibility is best accomplished by being involved. Each year our goal has been to assist as many organizations and events as possible through air time, news coverage, personal appearances, and volunteering. Many times we have asked you, our viewers, to get involved, either through donations or volunteering, and each time you have responded generously. We thank you for your contributions.

As we enter our next 50 years, things in our industry will change, our community will change, and our country will change. As a news organization we will be there to help you understand and adjust to those changes. We will provide information that you need and we will remain committed to providing it quickly and accurately.

The one thing that will not change in the next 50 years is our commitment to you and to the community. We will continue to be involved, we will continue to help when help is needed, and we will continue to care, because we are the station that cares for you.

History of KWQC-TV6

It was October 31, 1949. KWQC-TV6 (then WOC-TV) signed on for its first official telecast day and was first to bring the "magic lantern" into the 400 homes with television sets here in the Quad Cities. Just 18 months before, the Palmer family, pioneers in radio, had announced plans for a proposed television station and had purchased the old Ed Ryan residence at 805 Brady Street to house the studios of both WOC radio and television. At that time, the Palmer family was confident that the new medium would become a reality within two years. Remodeling of the Ryan building was started a short time later, and an annex was added to the east side of the building. The annex provided office space on the second floor and a garage and maintenance area for the WOC mobile unit on the ground floor.

Initially all the programming on WOC originated in the studio, but in July 1950 some of the NBC network programs were added. Twelve microwave towers, each about 30 miles apart, made up a relay system between Chicago and Des Moines. NBC programming was pulled from one of the towers near Princeton, Iowa, and routed via the telephone exchange to the station. By September 30, 1950, a more robust NBC schedule, which included the World Series, was carried live on television. In 1956 NBC added color to its programming, but all locally originated programming was still black and white.

KWQC-TV6

In 1961 a new 1,000-foot transmission tower and building were constructed at Pleasant Valley. On June 7, 1962, ground was broken on the north side of the Ryan building for a new, more luxurious studio facility. In 1963 construction of the new studio was completed; by September 1963, operations moved from the old Ryan building to the new building. The Ryan residence was leveled a short time later, but the exterior of the annex remained and was resurfaced in brick to match the new building. Today the annex houses station vehicles and NBC satellite gear.

In 1964 film programs that were available were broadcast in color, and 2-inch videotape machines were part of the broadcast plant. By 1967 all locally originated programming was in full color. In 1982 a new 1,400-foot tower and antenna were erected to replace the old 1,000-foot tower. In 1985 the studio and transmitter were revamped to add stereo audio.

In 1986 the Palmer family split their Quad Cities radio and television holdings, and KWQC-TV6 was born. Broad Street Television purchased KWQC-TV6 from Palmer Communications in 1989, and in April 1996 KWQC-TV6 became part of Young Broadcasting Incorporated.

The song "Hello, Quad Cities" was introduced to the Quad Cities by KWQC-TV6 in the early 1990s. The lyrics were written by KWQC-TV6 employees to express the station's strong alliance with the community and the viewers.

Hello, Quad Cities

There's a feeling in the air
That you can't get anywhere
Except the Quad Cities.

And no matter where we go
The best people that we know
Are in the Quad Cities.

Where people show they care
TV6 is always there,
Standing by their side.

From where the rivers flow,
To the hometowns we know,
Friends and neighbors building pride.

Chorus

Making a difference where we go
KWQC says HELLO,
Hello Iowa,
Hello Illinois,
TV6 cares for you!

Acknowledgments

Cookbook Coordinator
Trish Tague

Additional Assistance
Shelli Tague
Cathie Whiteside
Mary Ann Zack

Contributors
Helen Agnew
Jonathan Banfield
Rick Benjamin
Pat Berger
Doug Bierman
Jeff Bilyeu
Tom Brokaw
Theresa Bryant
Mrs. George Bush
Steve Butler
Mrs. Jimmy Carter
Shannon Colgan
Thom Cornelis
Jason DeRusha
Sharon DeRycke
John Elway
James Folkers
Leeza Gibbons
Jeff Glass
Sydney Gohring
Jim Graham
Bret Hamilton
Hal Hart
Amy Hatfield
John Hegeman
Wendi Henningsen
Jim Heubach
Frank Husemann
JoAnn Johnson

Mrs. Lyndon Johnson
Drew Jones
Sue Ketelsen
Charles King
Priscilla Kraft
Carol LeBeau
Jay Leno
Marcia Lense
Erik Maitland
Jill Martens
Ken McFarland
Gary Metivier
Mike Mickle
John Mooney
Jennifer Oetzmann
Mike Ortiz
Ivan Owens
Karen Peacock
Dan Pearson
Beth Perry
Mrs. Richard Petty
Heidi Plummer
Mrs. Ronald Reagan
Doug Retherford
Fran Riley
Sheldon Ripson
Al Roker
Paula Sands
Tom Schrad
Kurt Schreiner
Teresa Seffel
Jason Shoultz
Kathy Sidlinger
Sean Smith
Dave Stark
Hank Strunk
Sara Strunk
Patricia Sundine-Edward
Terry Swails
Shelli Tague
Trish Tague
Tim Thompson
Dave VanMeter
Betty Vesey
Louanne Walters
Teddy Wazac
Cathie Whiteside
Allen Wiese
Chris Zack
Ed Zack
Mary Ann Zack
Andrea Zinga

Appetizers & Snacks

Erik Maitland

Jason DeRusha

Dan Pearson

Thom Cornelis

KWQC-TV6

Workplace Olympics challenges individuals to some pretty tough assignments!

The United Way of the Quad Cities is an important part of the community. Each year the United Way raises and allocates funds for many programs that serve families, youth, and seniors in the Quad City region. Through a careful selection process, the United Way works with local agencies to ensure that funds are used to best benefit the needs of the community.

KWQC-TV6

United Way's annual campaign is a way that Quad Citians can make contributions either through their workplace or on their own and be assured that their money will be used to meet the needs of the community. United Way also has several "fun-raisers" during the annual campaign, including the Workplace Olympics and the Mid-Term Report.

The "Mid-Term" Party gives the cheerleaders a chance to show off their spirit!

Appetizers & Snacks

Quick-and-Easy Bean Dip

2 teaspoons vegetable oil
1 small onion, chopped
1 clove of garlic, minced
1 (16-ounce) can pork and beans
½ teaspoon Worcestershire sauce, or to taste
2 dashes of Tabasco sauce, or to taste
1 jalapeño, seeded, sliced

✦ Heat the oil in a saucepan over medium-high heat. Add the onion and garlic.

✦ Sauté until the onion is translucent. Add the pork and beans; mash the beans with a fork. Stir the mixture until well combined. Cook for 5 minutes.

✦ Add the Worcestershire sauce and Tabasco sauce; mix well. Simmer over low heat for 10 to 15 minutes or until heated through.

✦ Transfer the mixture to a serving bowl and top with sliced jalapeño.

✦ Yield: 1½ cups

Dateline April 1939—President Franklin D. Roosevelt opened the New York World's Fair with a telecast—the debut of television. By 1947, there were still only nine television stations in operation, but there were applications before the Federal Communications Commission to construct others. Dr. B. J. Palmer was one of those applying for permission; his new venture would be called WOC-TV.

The generosity of our viewers is incredible. Year after year, KWQC-TV6 viewers have given generously to a wide variety of organizations, such as Easter Seals, that are in need of funds.

Spicy Bean Dip

1 (31-ounce) can refried beans

3 tablespoons (about) milk

6 ounces Mexican Velveeta cheese, cubed

2 tablespoons hot taco sauce, or to taste

1 tablespoon chili powder, or to taste

✦ Place the refried beans in a saucepan. Add the milk; mix well. Cook over low heat until heated through, stirring occasionally.

✦ Add the cheese. Cook until the cheese is melted, stirring constantly. Add the taco sauce and chili powder; mix well.

✦ Serve warm with tortilla chips for dipping.

✦ May instead be prepared in a slow cooker. May add 8 ounces browned ground beef to serve as a main dish.

✦ Yield: 3 cups

Each year KWQC-TV6 and our viewers are involved in a variety of community events throughout eastern Iowa and western Illinois. Favorite summertime events include the fairs and festivals held throughout the region. From the rough-riding rodeo at the New Windsor Fair & Rodeo to the toe-tapping country music and the grandeur of the horses at the Mississippi Valley Fair, Quad Citians know how to enjoy summertime.

Company Cheese Ball

12 slices bacon, chopped

1 bunch green onions, chopped

1 rib celery, chopped

½ green bell pepper, chopped

½ red bell pepper, chopped

1 teaspoon prepared horseradish

16 ounces cream cheese, softened

✦ Fry the bacon pieces in a skillet over medium-high heat until crisp; drain on paper towels.

✦ Combine the bacon pieces, green onions, celery, green pepper, red pepper, horseradish and cream cheese in a bowl; mix well.

✦ Shape the mixture into a ball; cover with plastic wrap and refrigerate for 12 hours.

✦ Garnish the cheese ball with paprika or chopped parsley.

✦ Yield: 10 to 20 servings

Holiday Torta

16 ounces light cream cheese, softened

1 envelope ranch salad dressing mix

1 (6-ounce) jar marinated artichoke hearts, drained, chopped

3 tablespoons minced fresh parsley

⅓ cup chopped roasted red bell peppers

✦ Combine the cream cheese and salad dressing mix in a large bowl; mix well.

✦ Combine the artichoke hearts, parsley and red peppers in a medium mixer bowl; mix well.

✦ Line a 3-cup bowl with plastic wrap. Alternate layers of cream cheese and vegetables in a bowl, beginning and ending with a cream cheese layer. Chill for 4 hours.

✦ Invert the torta onto a serving plate. Remove the plastic wrap.

✦ Garnish with Bibb lettuce, red bell pepper strips and parsley. Serve with assorted crackers.

✦ Yield: 10 to 12 servings

The Best Spinach Dip Ever

3 green onions, finely chopped

1 (10-ounce) package frozen spinach, thawed, drained

1 envelope vegetable soup mix

1 cup sour cream

1½ cups mayonnaise

✦ Combine the green onions, spinach, soup mix, sour cream and mayonnaise in a mixer bowl; mix well.

✦ Transfer the mixture to a serving bowl. Chill, covered, for 3 hours.

✦ Serve with bread or crackers.

✦ Yield: 30 servings

Jason DeRusha
KWQC-TV6 Anchor

The KWQC-TV6 Women's Lifestyles Fair is an annual spring event in the Quad Cities. Each year thousands attend and enjoy seminars, displays, fashion shows, and special appearances by such celebrities as Richard Simmons, Martha Stewart, Faith Daniels, Robert Kelker-Kelly, Mr. Food, Kristian Alphonso, and Peter Reckell.

Roasted Garlic

1 bulb of garlic

1 tablespoon extra-virgin olive oil

1 teaspoon balsamic vinegar

⅛ teaspoon salt (optional)

✦ Preheat the oven to 350 degrees. Cut a thin slice off the top of the garlic bulb, exposing the cloves.

✦ Blend the olive oil, vinegar and salt in a small bowl. Dip the garlic bulb in the mixture, completely coating it with oil.

✦ Wrap the garlic bulb in foil. Bake for 1 hour or until the cloves are soft and golden brown.

✦ To serve, remove the cloves from the skin and spread on toasted Italian bread slices.

✦ To serve as a dip, mix peeled garlic cloves with 8 ounces softened cream cheese; add 1 tablespoon chopped fresh herbs or crushed nuts and mix thoroughly.

✦ Yield: 8 to 10 servings

Theresa Bryant
KWQC-TV6 Weather Anchor

Granola

4 cups old-fashioned rolled oats

1 cup shredded coconut

1 cup chopped pine nuts or walnuts

1 cup wheat germ

⅓ cup sesame seeds

½ cup vegetable oil

½ cup honey

3 cups chopped dried fruit such as dates, prunes and raisins

✦ Preheat the oven to 325 degrees. Combine the oats, coconut, pine nuts, wheat germ and sesame seeds in a large bowl; mix well.

✦ Boil the oil and honey in a saucepan over medium-high heat. Pour into the oat mixture; mix well.

✦ Spread the mixture evenly in two 10x15-inch baking pans.

✦ Bake for 25 minutes, stirring occasionally. Remove from the oven and add the fruit; mix well.

✦ Yield: 1½ pounds

Tom Brokaw
"NBC Nightly News" *Anchor*

Portobello Mushrooms in Cognac

1 tablespoon extra-virgin olive oil

½ cup chicken broth

2 cloves of garlic, minced

1 shallot, minced

1 tablespoon chopped fresh parsley

1 tablespoon chopped fresh basil

1 tablespoon chopped fresh chives

Salt and pepper to taste

¼ cup Cognac

4 large portobello mushrooms

✦ Preheat the oven to 450 degrees. Heat the olive oil and chicken broth in a saucepan over medium heat.

✦ Add the garlic, shallot, parsley, basil, chives, salt and pepper. Cook for 3 minutes, stirring occasionally.

✦ Add the Cognac. Simmer for 5 minutes.

✦ Arrange the mushrooms smooth-side down in an ungreased baking dish. Pour the Cognac mixture over the mushrooms, filling the caps.

✦ Bake for 15 minutes or until the mushrooms are tender when pierced with a fork. Serve on a bed of colorful greens.

✦ Yield: 4 servings

Theresa Bryant
KWQC-TV6 Weather Anchor

Miniature Cheeseburgers

1 cup margarine, softened

1 teaspoon poppy seeds

½ teaspoon onion powder

½ teaspoon garlic salt

½ teaspoon dried basil

12 ounces ground beef

1 egg

Salt and freshly ground pepper to taste

60 miniature party rolls

60 slices American or Swiss cheese

✦ Preheat the oven to 350 degrees. Cream the margarine, poppy seeds, onion powder, garlic salt and basil in a mixer bowl until light and fluffy; set aside.

✦ Combine the ground beef, egg, salt and pepper in a bowl; mix thoroughly.

✦ Slice each roll into halves horizontally. If the package of rolls is frozen, you can slice the package as one, leaving the rolls attached.

✦ Spread the cut surface of each roll with the margarine mixture. Place a teaspoon of the ground beef mixture in the center of each bottom half. Top with a slice of cheese and the top of the roll. Wrap the rolls tightly in foil and freeze.

✦ Bake frozen wrapped rolls for 35 to 40 minutes or until ground beef is cooked through.

✦ Serve hot.

✦ Yield: 15 to 20 servings

Uncle Louie's Chicken Wings Marinara

24 to 36 chicken wings

½ cup olive oil

2 teaspoons minced garlic, or ½ teaspoon garlic powder

1 (28-ounce) can whole Italian-style tomatoes

1 tablespoon chopped parsley

Salt and pepper to taste

2 tablespoons Durkee hot sauce, or to taste

✦ Preheat the broiler. Broil the chicken wings on a rack in a broiler pan until cooked through. Heat the olive oil and garlic in a saucepan over medium heat for 1 minute.

✦ Process the tomatoes through a sieve or food mill; add to the garlic mixture.

✦ Add the parsley, salt and pepper. Cook for 20 minutes.

✦ Add the hot sauce. Cook for 3 to 4 minutes.

✦ Toss the chicken wings with ½ cup of the sauce in a serving bowl. Serve the remaining sauce on the side for dipping.

✦ Yield: 24 to 36 servings

Jay Leno
NBC "Tonight Show" *Host*

Wieners in Barbecue Sauce

1 (18-ounce) jar Cookies barbecue sauce

1 (18-ounce) jar smoke-flavored barbecue sauce

1 (16-ounce) package miniature frankfurters

1 (16-ounce) package miniature smoked frankfurters

1 (16-ounce) package Polish sausage, cut into bite-size pieces

1 (16-ounce) package smoked sausage, cut into bite-size pieces

✦ Combine the Cookies barbecue sauce, smoke-flavored barbecue sauce, frankfurters, smoked frankfurters, Polish sausage and smoked sausage in a large saucepan.

✦ Simmer over medium heat for 1 hour, stirring occasionally.

✦ Yield: 30 to 40 servings

Soups, Salads & Side Dishes

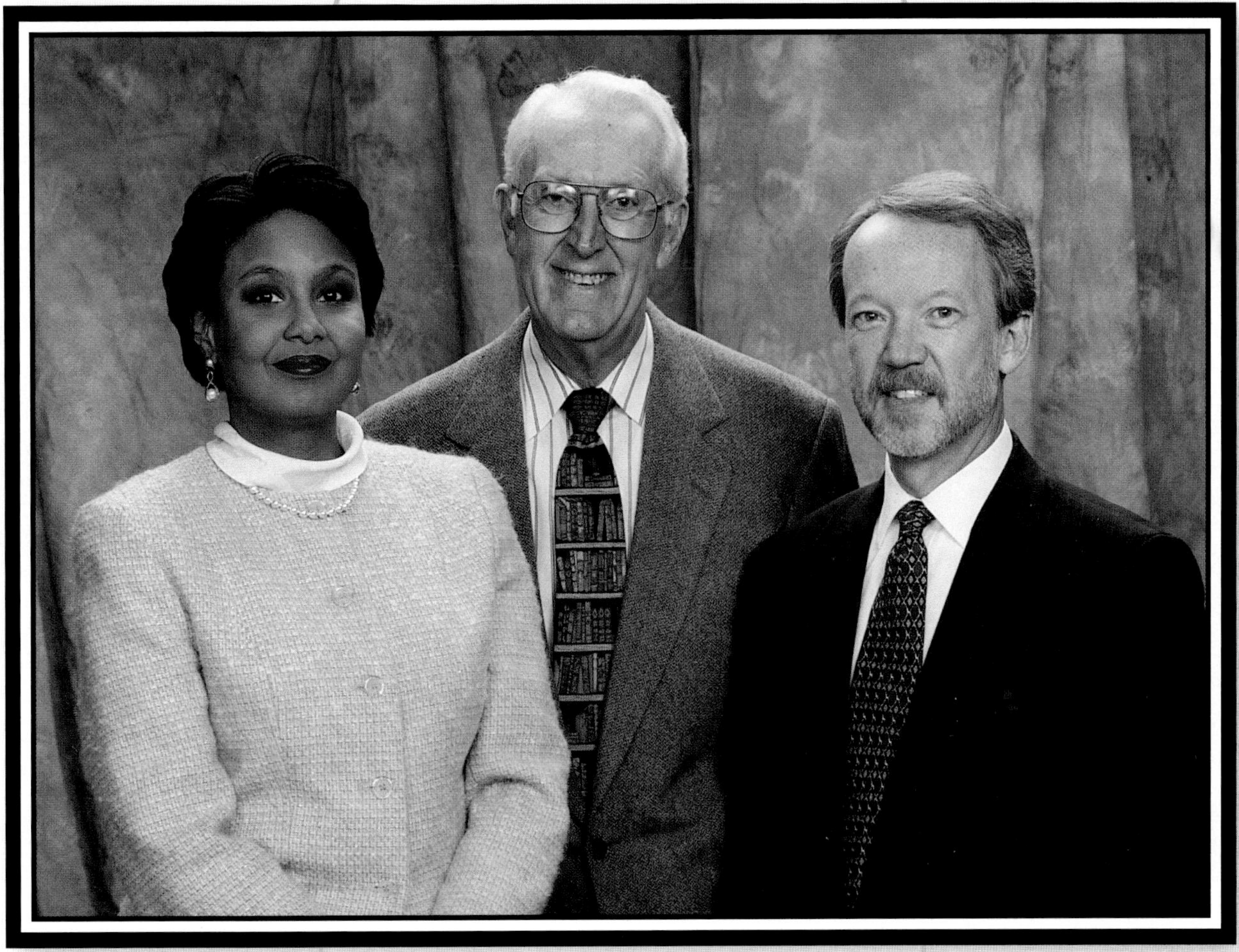

Theresa Bryant

Charles King

Jim Victor

The Runway To The Cure Luncheon began in 1995 as the kickoff event for the annual Women's Lifestyles Fair. The proceeds from the style show benefit the Susan G. Komen Quad Cities Race For The Cure®. The style show features career and dressy clothes along with casual and cruise attire, with some clothes modeled by local breast cancer survivors. Celebrity speakers for this event have included Gary Collins and his wife, Mary Ann Mobley, and Jill Eikenberry and her husband, Michael Tucker.

KWQC-TV6

The annual Susan G. Komen Quad Cities Race For The Cure® was first run in 1990 at Bettendorf High School. The race recently completed its ninth year and brought over 8,000 runners and walkers together on Arsenal Island to help fund the Quad Cities' fight against breast cancer. The race is presented locally by Genesis Medical Center, Junior League of the Quad Cities, and KWQC-TV6.

KWQC-TV6

Soups, Salads & Side Dishes

Cream of Broccoli Soup—With No Cream

1 tablespoon vegetable oil

1 medium onion, chopped

1 clove of garlic, crushed

1 bay leaf

1 pound broccoli, chopped

2½ cups vegetable stock or chicken stock

½ cup mashed cooked potatoes

Salt and pepper to taste

Juice of ½ lemon

¼ cup plain yogurt or sour cream

✦ Heat the oil in a large saucepan over medium-high heat. Add the onion, garlic and bay leaf. Sauté for 4 minutes or until the onion is translucent.

✦ Stir in the broccoli, vegetable stock and potatoes. Simmer, covered, for 10 minutes or until the broccoli is tender but still bright green. Remove and discard the bay leaf. Cool slightly.

✦ Transfer the soup to a blender container. Add the salt, pepper and lemon juice. Process until almost smooth.

✦ Ladle into bowls. Place a dollop of yogurt in the center of each bowl just before serving.

✦ Yield: 4 servings

Mrs. Jimmy Carter
Wife of President Jimmy Carter

In July 1949, it was estimated that 300 homes in the Quad Cities had a television set. Reception was possible only during freak conditions.

Cauliflower and Cheese Soup

1 quart water
2 medium onions, chopped
2 carrots, chopped
2 teaspoons dried basil
1 teaspoon salt
½ teaspoon freshly ground pepper
2 cups broccoli florets
5 to 6 cups chopped cauliflower
¼ cup butter
¼ cup flour
2 (10-ounce) cans chicken broth, heated
1 quart milk
2 (10-ounce) cans cream of Cheddar soup

✦ Bring the water, onions, carrots, basil, salt and pepper to a boil in a 6-quart stockpot over high heat. Reduce the heat. Simmer, covered, for 5 minutes.

✦ Add the broccoli and cauliflower. Simmer, covered, for 15 minutes.

✦ Melt the butter in a large saucepan over medium heat. Stir in the flour. Cook for 1 to 2 minutes or until the mixture thickens, whisking constantly. Add the hot chicken broth gradually, whisking constantly. Pour into the cauliflower mixture.

✦ Combine the milk and Cheddar soup in the saucepan used for the broth; mix well. Pour into the stockpot with the cauliflower.

✦ Heat until steaming. Serve immediately.

✦ Yield: 20 to 24 servings

Iowa's Corn Chowder

1 tablespoon vegetable oil

1 small onion, chopped

3 (17-ounce) cans cream-style corn

3 cups milk

2 cups mashed cooked potatoes

Salt and pepper to taste

4 slices bacon, cooked, crumbled

✦ Heat the oil in a large saucepan over medium-high heat. Add the onion. Sauté until the onion is translucent.

✦ Add the corn, milk, potatoes, salt and pepper; stir to combine. Cook over low heat for 15 minutes, stirring occasionally.

✦ Add the crumbled bacon. Serve immediately.

✦ Yield: 8 to 10 servings

"Mr. Weatherwise," a popular local program, debuted in 1949. The Mr. Weatherwise puppet was created by the WOC-TV production staff to give weather information in a humorous but authoritative manner. The show aired from 6:55 to 7:00 p.m., Monday through Friday.

Thom Cornelis

French Onion Soup

2 tablespoons butter
2 large Bermuda onions, sliced
1 tablespoon flour
2 quarts beef stock
1 cup dry white wine
Salt and pepper to taste
8 slices French bread, toasted
8 slices Swiss cheese
2 tablespoons grated Parmesan cheese

✦ Heat the butter in a large saucepan over medium heat. Add the onions. Sauté for 30 minutes or until the onions are translucent.

✦ Sprinkle the flour over the onions. Cook for 1 minute, stirring constantly with a wooden spoon.

✦ Add the beef stock, wine, salt and pepper gradually. Simmer for 15 minutes, stirring occasionally.

✦ Preheat the broiler. Pour the hot soup into individual heatproof soup bowls. Place a slice of French bread on top of each serving. Cover with a slice of Swiss cheese and sprinkle the top with Parmesan cheese.

✦ Place the bowls under the broiler for 1 minute or until the cheese is melted. Serve immediately.

✦ Yield: 8 servings

Thom Cornelis
KWQC-TV6 Sports Anchor

Super Bowl Soup with Barley, Beans and Beer

2½ cups water

1 tablespoon butter

8 ounces barley

2 pounds lean ground beef

½ cup chopped onion

2 (19-ounce) cans red kidney beans, drained

3 (14-ounce) cans peeled tomatoes

1 (12-ounce) can beer

Salt and pepper to taste

½ teaspoon garlic powder, or to taste

1 teaspoon chili powder, or to taste

✦ Bring the water to a boil in a saucepan over high heat. Stir in the butter and barley.

✦ Reduce the heat to low. Cook, covered, for 35 to 40 minutes or until the barley is tender.

✦ Brown the ground beef and onion in a large skillet, stirring until the ground beef is crumbly; drain well. Transfer to a 10-quart stockpot.

✦ Add the barley, beans, undrained tomatoes, beer, salt, pepper, garlic powder and chili powder; mix well.

✦ Cook over medium-low heat for 10 minutes or until the beer evaporates.

✦ Yield: 8 servings

KWQC-TV6

Ground Beef Soup

2 tablespoons butter
1 cup chopped onion
1 clove of garlic, minced
2½ pounds ground beef
3 (10-ounce) cans beef stock
1 (10-ounce) can tomatoes with green chiles
1 (8-ounce) can tomato sauce
1 cup chopped unpeeled potatoes
1 cup chopped carrots
1 cup chopped celery
1 (16-ounce) can French-style green beans
1 cup dry red wine
1 tablespoon chopped parsley
½ teaspoon dried basil
Salt and pepper to taste

✦ Heat the butter in a large saucepan over medium-high heat. Add the onion and garlic. Sauté until the onion is translucent.

✦ Brown the ground beef in a large skillet, stirring until crumbly; drain well. Add to the onion mixture.

✦ Add the beef stock, tomatoes with green chiles, tomato sauce, potatoes, carrots, celery, green beans, wine, parsley, basil, salt and pepper; mix well.

✦ Cook over medium-high heat for 15 minutes or until the vegetables are tender.

✦ Serve with warm bread.

✦ Yield: 8 servings

John Elway
Of the Denver Broncos

Almost Store-Bought Chili

1 pound ground beef
1 (15-ounce) can chili starter
1 (10-ounce) can diced tomatoes with green peppers and onions
1 (8-ounce) can tomato sauce
1 cup water
Pepper to taste
Garlic powder to taste

✦ Brown the ground beef in a skillet, stirring until crumbly; drain well.

✦ Add the chili starter, tomatoes with green peppers and onions, tomato sauce, water, pepper and garlic powder; mix well.

✦ Simmer over medium heat for 30 to 45 minutes.

✦ For the best flavor, refrigerate this chili for 24 hours. Reheat gently before serving.

✦ Yield: 5 to 6 servings

Marjorie Meinert and George Sontag were popular with WOC listeners and viewers in the 1950s.

White Chili

1 pound Great Northern beans, soaked, drained
6 cups water
1 tablespoon vegetable oil
3 large potatoes, peeled, chopped
1½ cups finely chopped onions
1 tablespoon minced garlic
1 (10-ounce) can chicken broth
1½ cups dry white wine or water
1 pound boneless skinless chicken breasts, cut into bite-size pieces
2 teaspoons chili powder, or to taste
1 teaspoon Tabasco sauce
2 teaspoons ground cumin, or to taste
Salt to taste
1 cup half-and-half
¾ cup shredded Cheddar cheese

✦ Place the beans in a large stockpot. Cover with water. Add the oil. Bring to a boil over high heat. Reduce the heat. Simmer, partially covered, for 2 hours or until tender.

✦ Combine the potatoes, onions, garlic, half the chicken broth and the wine in a large saucepan. Bring to a boil over high heat. Reduce the heat. Simmer for 30 minutes or until the potatoes are tender.

✦ Add the chicken and remaining chicken broth. Add the chili powder, Tabasco sauce, cumin and salt. Cook over medium heat for 20 minutes or until the chicken is cooked through.

✦ Add the drained cooked beans, half-and-half and Cheddar cheese; mix well.

✦ Ladle into bowls. Garnish each serving with sour cream, shredded cheese, chopped onions, sliced jalapeños and chopped green bell pepper.

✦ Yield: 12 servings

Andrea Zinga
Former WOC Reporter

Clam Chowder

½ cup margarine
1 large onion, chopped
2 large potatoes, peeled, chopped
1 (8-ounce) can clams
½ cup water
Salt and pepper to taste
6 tablespoons flour
6 cups milk
8 ounces sliced Velveeta cheese, or mixed Cheddar and Velveeta cheeses

✦ Melt the margarine in a large saucepan over medium-high heat. Add the onion, potatoes, undrained clams and water. Cook for 10 minutes or until the potatoes are tender. Add the salt and pepper.

✦ Combine the flour and milk in a small bowl. Whisk until the mixture is smooth. Pour into the soup.

✦ Add the cheese. Cook until the cheese is melted and the soup is hot, stirring constantly.

✦ Yield: 8 to 10 servings

This studio shot is from the original WOC studio in the early 1950s.

Seafood Bisque

½ cup butter

½ cup flour

½ cup crab stock, lobster stock or bottled clam juice

1 cup corn kernels

1 cup whipping cream

8 ounces crab meat or lobster meat

Salt and pepper to taste

✦ Melt the butter in a 5-quart saucepan over medium-high heat. Add the flour. Cook for 2 minutes or until the foam subsides, whisking constantly.

✦ Whisk in the crab stock. Bring to a boil, whisking constantly. Reduce the heat. Simmer for 20 minutes.

✦ Stir in the corn. Cook for 20 minutes. Add the whipping cream, stirring constantly. Add the crab meat, salt and pepper; mix well.

✦ Remove the pan from the heat. Let stand for 10 minutes.

✦ Garnish each serving with chopped fresh scallions, if desired.

✦ Note: To prepare homemade crab stock or lobster stock, combine 2 quarts water and 2 quartered onions in a large stockpot. Add 5 medium hard-shell crabs or 2 medium lobster tails. Cook for 45 minutes. Strain the stock before using.

✦ Yield: 4 to 6 servings

Terry Swails

Rose's Apricot-Pineapple Salad

1 (29-ounce) can apricot halves

1 (29-ounce) can crushed pineapple

¾ cup miniature marshmallows

1 (3-ounce) package orange gelatin

1 (3-ounce) package lemon gelatin

2 cups boiling water

½ cup sugar

1 tablespoon flour

1 egg, slightly beaten

2 tablespoons butter

1 cup whipping cream, whipped

✦ For the gelatin, drain the apricots and pineapple, reserving 1 cup apricot juice and 1 cup pineapple juice. Cut the apricots into small pieces. Combine the apricots, pineapple and marshmallows in a bowl; set aside.

✦ Combine the orange and lemon gelatins in a large bowl. Add the boiling water, stirring until the gelatin is dissolved.

✦ Add ½ cup of the reserved apricot juice and ½ cup of the reserved pineapple juice to the gelatin, stirring constantly. Chill for 20 minutes or until the mixture thickens but is not firm.

✦ Fold the marshmallow mixture into the gelatin. Pour the mixture into a 9x13-inch pan. Chill until firm.

✦ For the topping, combine the sugar and flour in a saucepan. Stir in the egg. Add the remaining ½ cup apricot juice and ½ cup pineapple juice gradually, stirring constantly.

✦ Cook over low heat for 5 minutes or until thickened, stirring constantly. Remove from the heat and stir in the butter.

✦ Cool the mixture completely. Fold in the whipped cream. Spread the mixture over the firm gelatin. Serve immediately.

✦ Yield: 10 to 12 servings

Terry Swails
KWQC-TV6 Chief Meteorologist

Seven-Layer Salad

1 head iceberg lettuce, shredded

½ cup chopped celery

½ cup chopped green bell pepper

½ cup chopped onion

1 (10-ounce) package frozen peas, cooked, drained

2 cups mayonnaise

2 tablespoons sugar

1 cup shredded Cheddar cheese

8 slices bacon, cooked, crumbled

✦ Arrange the lettuce in a glass bowl or dish. Combine the celery, green pepper and onion; mix well. Layer the celery mixture evenly over the lettuce.

✦ Layer the peas over the celery mixture. Spread mayonnaise over the peas. Sprinkle with the sugar.

✦ Layer the cheese over the top. Sprinkle with the crumbled bacon.

✦ Cover the salad tightly with plastic wrap. Chill for 8 hours or overnight.

✦ The salad will stay crisp in the refrigerator for several days.

✦ Yield: 18 servings

Mom's Quick Taco Salad

- 1 cup prepared ranch salad dressing
- 1 envelope taco seasoning mix
- 1 head iceberg lettuce, shredded
- 3 tomatoes, sliced
- 1 (16-ounce) can red kidney beans
- ¾ cup shredded Cheddar cheese
- 1 cup crushed taco chips

✦ Combine the salad dressing and taco seasoning mix in a small bowl; mix well. Set aside.

✦ Toss the lettuce, tomatoes and beans in a large bowl. Pour the dressing over the vegetables.

✦ Add the cheese and chips. Toss gently. Serve immediately.

✦ Yield: 8 servings

Jason Shoultz
KWQC-TV6 Reporter

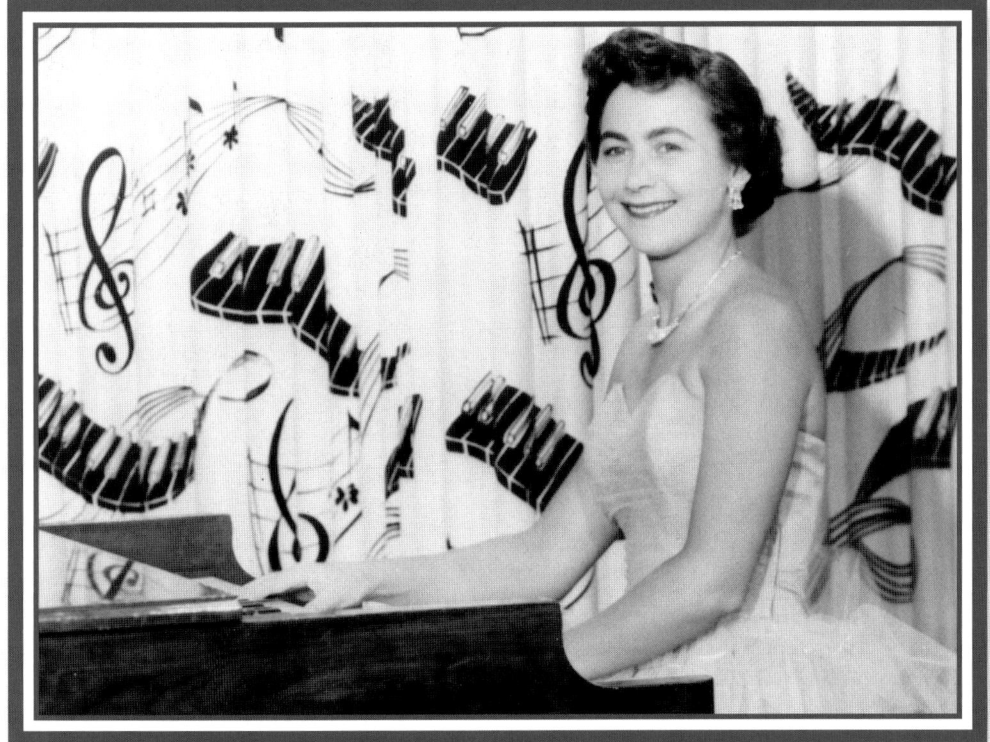

Marjorie Meinert performed in "Musical Moods" in the early 1950s.

That Good Salad

½ cup olive oil
3 tablespoons lemon juice
1 large clove of garlic, minced
½ teaspoon salt
½ teaspoon pepper
1 head romaine lettuce, torn into pieces
2 cups cherry tomatoes, or 1 cup chopped tomatoes
1 cup shredded Swiss cheese
⅔ cup slivered almonds
½ cup grated Parmesan cheese
8 slices bacon, cooked, crumbled
1 cup Caesar-flavored croutons

✦ For the dressing, combine the olive oil, lemon juice, garlic, salt and pepper in a glass jar with a tight-fitting lid. Cover the jar and shake until the ingredients are well mixed. Chill thoroughly.

✦ For the salad, combine the lettuce, tomatoes, Swiss cheese, almonds, Parmesan cheese, crumbled bacon and croutons in a large bowl. Toss to mix well.

✦ Pour the chilled dressing over the salad and toss to coat. Serve immediately.

✦ Yield: 2 to 6 servings

Mom's Fantastic Baked Beans

6 to 8 slices bacon, chopped
¼ cup chopped onion
1 (16-ounce) can pork and beans
½ cup packed light brown sugar
1 cup catsup

✦ Cook the bacon and onion in a large skillet over medium-high heat for 5 minutes or until the bacon is cooked through; do not drain.

✦ Add the pork and beans, brown sugar and catsup. Simmer for 15 minutes. Serve immediately.

✦ Yield: 5 servings

Jason Shoultz
KWQC-TV6 Reporter

Lemon Potatoes

10 to 15 new potatoes, scrubbed

2 tablespoons butter

1 tablespoon extra-virgin olive oil

⅔ cup freshly squeezed lemon juice

½ teaspoon grated lemon peel

1 tablespoon chopped parsley

1 tablespoon chopped fresh chives

1 tablespoon chopped fresh basil

½ teaspoon Mrs. Dash seasoning (optional)

✦ Boil the potatoes in water to cover in a saucepan until tender; drain. Transfer to a large bowl; set aside.

✦ Combine the butter and olive oil in a saucepan. Add the lemon juice. Cook over medium heat for 3 minutes or until the mixture is heated through, stirring occasionally.

✦ Add the lemon peel, parsley, chives, basil and Mrs. Dash seasoning to the butter mixture. Cook for 1 minute, stirring constantly.

✦ Pour the lemon juice mixture over the potatoes. Toss to coat the potatoes thoroughly.

✦ Yield: 4 to 6 servings

Theresa Bryant
KWQC-TV6 Weather Anchor

Mike Mickle

Easy Potatoes au Gratin

2 (16-ounce) packages frozen hash brown potatoes

½ cup melted butter

1 (10-ounce) can cream of chicken soup

2 cups sour cream

2 cups shredded American cheese

2 tablespoons minced onion

1 teaspoon salt

½ teaspoon pepper

✦ Preheat the oven to 350 degrees. Combine the potatoes, butter, soup, sour cream, cheese, onion, salt and pepper in a large bowl; mix well.

✦ Pour the potato mixture into a greased 9x13-inch baking dish. Bake for 1 hour or until brown and bubbly.

✦ Yield: 4 to 6 servings

Mike Mickle
KWQC-TV6 Anchor

Zucchini Casserole

4 medium zucchini
Salt to taste
6 tablespoons butter or margarine
¾ cup shredded carrots
½ cup chopped onion
2½ cups seasoned croutons, or cubed stuffing mix
1 (10-ounce) can cream of chicken soup
½ cup sour cream
1 tablespoon butter

✦ Preheat the oven to 350 degrees. Peel and slice the zucchini into ½-inch slices.

✦ Cook the zucchini in salted water to cover in a saucepan for 2 to 3 minutes or until tender. Drain and set aside.

✦ Melt 6 tablespoons butter in a large skillet over medium-high heat. Add the carrots and onion. Sauté for 3 to 4 minutes or until tender-crisp.

✦ Stir in the croutons. Fold in the soup, sour cream and zucchini.

✦ Transfer the mixture to a greased 1½-quart casserole. Dot with 1 tablespoon butter. Bake for 30 to 40 minutes or until bubbly.

✦ Yield: 6 servings

The "Buck-Fifty"

1 (3-ounce) package ramen noodles, crumbled (any flavor)

1 (16-ounce) can corn kernels

1 (16-ounce) can sliced potatoes

Salt and pepper to taste

✦ Cook the noodles according to the package directions; drain.

✦ Combine the noodles, corn and potatoes in a saucepan. Cook over medium heat for 10 minutes, stirring occasionally.

✦ Add the contents of the noodle seasoning packet; mix well. Season with salt and pepper. Serve immediately.

✦ Yield: 2 servings

Cranberry Relish

1 (12-ounce) package fresh cranberries

1 large navel orange, peeled, cut into eighths

1 cup sugar

3 to 4 sprigs of mint, chopped

2 teaspoons cayenne

✦ Rinse and sort the cranberries. Combine the cranberries, orange, sugar, mint and cayenne in the bowl of a food processor.

✦ Process until the mixture is chunky by pulsing on and off. Transfer to a serving bowl. Garnish with mint leaves.

✦ Yield: 4 servings

Al Roker
NBC "Today Show" *Weather Anchor*

Breads & Brunch

Erik Maitland

Fran Riley

KWQC-TV6

Junior Achievement of the Quad Cities Area, Inc., educates young people about free enterprise and using business and economics to improve their lives. During the 1997-98 school year, more than 33,000 students throughout the 21-county Junior Achievement region participated in this unique business/education partnership. More than 1,500 volunteer "teachers" from the business communities utilize JA materials in the classroom to help ensure that every child in America has a fundamental understanding of the free enterprise system.

KWQC-TV6

The Student Hunger Drive is just one example of young people coming together to make the community a better place. Through the efforts of local high school students, thousands of pounds of food items are collected each fall and donated to area food pantries.

KWQC-TV6

Breads & Brunch

Banana Bread

½ cup milk
1 teaspoon vinegar
1 teaspoon baking soda
½ cup butter, softened
1½ cups sugar
2 eggs
½ teaspoon salt
2 cups unbleached flour
2½ medium bananas, peeled, mashed
½ cup chopped pecans or walnuts (optional)

✦ Preheat the oven to 300 degrees. Combine the milk, vinegar and baking soda in a bowl; set aside.

✦ Cream the butter and sugar in a mixer bowl until light and fluffy. Add the eggs and salt. Beat until smooth.

✦ Add the milk mixture and flour alternately to the creamed mixture, mixing well after each addition. Add the bananas and pecans. Beat for 2 minutes or until well mixed.

✦ Pour into a greased and floured loaf pan. Bake for 1½ hours or until loaf tests done.

✦ Yield: 1 loaf

The first test pattern sent from WOC in September 1949 was received in Cedar Rapids, Galesburg, Pekin, Savanna, Aledo, and Peoria. In October of 1949, it was reported that the test pattern was received in Iowa City and in Hannibal, Missouri.

Area children enjoyed free pony rides with "Wrangler Pete" Vagenas of the Circle 6 Ranch. "Wrangler Pete" was on the air during the early 1950s.

Poppy Seed Bread

1 (2-layer) package yellow cake mix

1 package coconut instant pudding mix

4 eggs

½ cup vegetable oil

1 cup hot water

¼ cup poppy seeds

✦ Preheat the oven to 350 degrees. Combine the cake mix, pudding mix, eggs, oil, water and poppy seeds in a mixer bowl. Beat at medium speed until smooth.

✦ Pour into a greased and floured loaf pan. Bake for 30 to 40 minutes or until loaf tests done.

✦ Yield: 1 loaf

Dan Pearson
KWQC-TV6 Anchor

Eddie Forest, "The Singing Sheriff," in the early 1950s.

Prune Bread

1 pound pitted prunes, chopped

2 cups water

¾ cup shortening or margarine

2 cups sugar

2 teaspoons ground cinnamon

1 teaspoon ground cloves

1 teaspoon grated nutmeg

3 eggs, beaten

1 teaspoon salt

2 teaspoons baking soda

1 teaspoon baking powder

4 cups flour

✦ Combine the prunes and water in a saucepan. Simmer over medium-high heat for 15 to 20 minutes.

✦ Add the shortening, sugar, cinnamon, cloves and nutmeg; mix well. Cook for 5 minutes.

✦ Remove from the heat and cool slightly. Add the eggs; mix well.

✦ Preheat the oven to 350 degrees. Sift the salt, baking soda, baking powder and flour together. Add to the prune mixture; mix well.

✦ Transfer the mixture to 2 greased loaf pans. Bake for 45 minutes or until the loaves test done.

✦ Yield: 2 loaves

Holiday Pumpkin Bread

3½ cups flour

2 cups sugar

1 teaspoon baking soda

1 teaspoon salt

1 teaspoon ground cinnamon

½ teaspoon grated nutmeg

4 eggs, beaten

⅔ cup water

1 cup corn oil

2 cups canned pumpkin

✦ Preheat the oven to 350 degrees. Combine the flour, sugar, baking soda, salt, cinnamon and nutmeg in a large bowl.

✦ Combine the eggs, water, corn oil and pumpkin in a medium bowl; mix well. Pour into the flour mixture; mix until thoroughly combined.

✦ Pour the batter into 2 greased loaf pans. Bake for 1 hour or until the loaves test done.

✦ Yield: 2 loaves

In July of 1950 some of the NBC network programs were added.

Monkey Bread

¾ ounce cake yeast, or ¼ ounce dry yeast

½ cup lukewarm milk

2 eggs

3 tablespoons sugar

1 teaspoon salt

3½ cups flour

½ to ¾ cup milk

¾ cup butter, softened

1 cup melted butter

1 egg

✦ Dissolve the yeast in ½ cup lukewarm milk in a large bowl. Add 2 eggs. Beat until well combined.

✦ Combine the sugar, salt and flour in a bowl; mix well. Add to the milk mixture; mix well. Add enough of the remaining ½ to ¾ cup milk gradually to make a soft dough, mixing well after each addition. Cut in the softened butter until well blended.

✦ Knead the dough on a floured surface until smooth and elastic. Let rise, covered, in a warm place until doubled in bulk. Punch the dough down. Knead again. Let rise for 40 minutes.

✦ Preheat the oven to 375 degrees. Grease and flour two 9-inch ring molds. Transfer the dough to a floured board and shape into a log. Cut into 28 pieces. Shape each piece into a ball and roll in melted butter. Arrange 7 balls in each of the prepared ring molds, leaving space between each ball. Place remaining balls on top of gaps. Let rise, covered, until doubled in bulk.

✦ Beat the remaining egg in a small bowl. Brush the tops of the rolls with the egg. Bake for 15 minutes or until golden brown.

✦ Yield: 24 to 30 servings

Mrs. Ronald Reagan
Wife of President Ronald Reagan

Cinnamon Bubble Bread

½ cup sugar
½ teaspoon cinnamon
3 (5-count) cans buttermilk biscuits
½ cup margarine
¾ cup sugar
¾ teaspoon cinnamon

✦ Preheat the oven to 350 degrees. Mix ½ cup sugar and ½ teaspoon cinnamon in a small bowl.

✦ Cut the biscuit dough into quarters. Dip into the cinnamon sugar mixture.

✦ Layer the biscuit dough pieces in a greased and floured bundt pan or 9-inch round baking pan.

✦ Combine the margarine, ¾ cup sugar and ¾ teaspoon cinnamon in a saucepan. Cook over medium heat until the margarine is melted. Stir until the sugar is dissolved. Pour over the biscuit dough layers.

✦ Bake for 30 to 35 minutes or until golden brown. Cool in the pan for 5 minutes. Invert onto a serving plate. Serve warm.

✦ Yield: 15 servings

Beer Muffins

3 cups self-rising flour
1 tablespoon sugar
1 (12-ounce) can beer, room temperature
Melted butter

✦ Preheat the oven to 350 degrees. Combine the flour, sugar and beer in a mixer bowl; mix well.

✦ Pour the batter into lightly greased muffin cups. Bake for 45 minutes or until golden brown.

✦ Remove from the oven. Brush the tops of the muffins with melted butter.

✦ Yield: 12 servings

Wes Holly and his wife, Joy, singing in the WOC studios as part of the annual Salvation Army *Tree of Lights* promotion in the late 1950s.

Chocolate Chocolate Chip Banana Muffins

1½ cups flour
1 cup sugar
¼ cup baking cocoa
1 teaspoon baking soda
½ teaspoon salt
¼ teaspoon baking powder
1⅓ cups mashed bananas
⅓ cup vegetable oil
1 egg
1 cup chocolate chips

✦ Preheat the oven to 350 degrees. Combine the flour, sugar, baking cocoa, baking soda, salt and baking powder in a bowl and mix well.

✦ Combine the bananas, oil and egg in a small bowl; mix well. Add to the flour mixture, stirring just until moistened. Fold in the chocolate chips.

✦ Fill greased or paper-lined muffin cups ¾ full. Bake for 20 to 25 minutes or until muffins test done.

✦ Yield: 12 servings

Pat Sundine, host of "Especially for You," at a Doll Style parade in the late 1950s.

Frosted Cinnamon Rolls

1 package roll mix
½ cup butter, softened
⅔ cup sugar
1 tablespoon ground cinnamon
2 tablespoons sugar
2 cups confectioners' sugar
2 to 3 tablespoons milk
1 teaspoon vanilla extract
¼ cup butter, softened

✦ For the rolls, prepare the dough according to the package directions. Roll the dough into a 10x15-inch rectangle. Preheat the oven to 375 degrees.

✦ Spread ½ cup butter over the dough. Combine ⅔ cup sugar and cinnamon in a bowl; mix well. Sprinkle over the dough. Roll the dough as for a jelly roll. Cut into 12 slices.

✦ Arrange cut side down 1 inch apart on an ungreased baking sheet. Sprinkle the remaining 2 tablespoons sugar over the top. Bake for 20 to 30 minutes or until golden.

✦ For the frosting, combine the confectioners' sugar, milk, vanilla and ¼ cup butter in a mixer bowl. Beat until smooth. Spread over the warm rolls.

✦ Yield: 12 rolls

Dan Pearson
KWQC-TV6 Anchor

Cinnamon Rolls

¾ cup milk
¼ cup sugar
1 teaspoon salt
¼ cup shortening
1 envelope dry yeast
¼ cup lukewarm water
1 egg
3 to 4 cups flour
½ cup melted butter
1½ cups sugar
3 tablespoons ground cinnamon

✦ Scald the milk in a saucepan over high heat. Combine ¼ cup sugar, salt and shortening in a mixer bowl. Pour in the hot milk; mix well. Cool to about 80 degrees.

✦ Dissolve the yeast in the lukewarm water in a bowl. Add to the milk mixture; mix well. Add the egg; mix well. Add enough of the flour gradually to make a soft dough, mixing well after each addition.

✦ Knead on a floured surface until smooth and elastic. Place in a greased bowl, turning to coat the surface. Let rise, covered, in a warm place until doubled in bulk. Punch the dough down. Divide the dough into 2 equal portions. Roll 1 portion into a rectangle. Brush with melted butter.

✦ Combine 1½ cups sugar and cinnamon in a bowl. Sprinkle some of the cinnamon sugar mixture over the rectangle. Roll as for a jelly roll. Seal the edges. Cut into 1-inch slices.

✦ Arrange cut side down 1 inch apart in a greased baking pan. Brush the tops with melted butter and sprinkle with some of the cinnamon sugar mixture. Repeat the process with the remaining dough and cinnamon sugar mixture. Let rise, covered, in a warm place for 45 minutes or until doubled in bulk.

✦ Preheat the oven to 350 degrees. Bake for 20 to 25 minutes or until golden brown. Let cool. Frost with confectioners' sugar icing, if desired.

✦ Yield: 18 to 20 rolls

Dutch Apple Fritters

4 cups flour
1 teaspoon salt
2 envelopes dry yeast
1 teaspoon ground cinnamon
2 cups milk
1 egg, beaten
1 cup raisins (optional)
½ cup chopped dates (optional)
Vegetable oil for frying
4 apples, peeled, sliced
Confectioners' sugar

✦ Combine the flour, salt, yeast and cinnamon in a large mixer bowl; mix well. Add the milk, egg, raisins and dates.

✦ Beat until the batter is stiff enough to hold a spoon upright. Let rise, covered, for 1 hour.

✦ Preheat the oil to 350 degrees in a deep fryer. Cover each apple slice with batter. Cook in the hot oil until golden brown.

✦ Remove to paper towels to drain. Sprinkle with confectioners' sugar while still warm.

✦ Yield: 10 to 15 servings

Marcia Lense

Kolachkis

½ cup confectioners' sugar
2 cups flour
1 cup melted margarine
2 teaspoons vanilla extract
1 (21-ounce) can fruit filling, any flavor

✦ Preheat the oven to 350 degrees. Combine the confectioners' sugar and flour in a bowl; mix well.

✦ Pour the margarine into a large bowl. Add the flour mixture gradually, stirring constantly until well mixed. Add the vanilla; mix well.

✦ Knead on a floured surface until smooth and elastic. Pinch off pieces of dough and roll into 1-inch balls. Place on a baking sheet.

✦ Use the bottom of a small glass to press each ball into a disc with an indentation in the center. Fill the indentations with fruit filling.

✦ Bake for 12 to 15 minutes or until the edges are brown. Remove from the oven.

✦ Sift additional confectioners' sugar over the top when cooled, if desired.

✦ Yield: 36 servings

Marcia Lense
KWQC-TV6 Anchor

Apple Bars

2½ cups flour
1 teaspoon salt
¾ cup shortening
¼ cup margarine
1 egg yolk
Milk
6 cooking apples, sliced
1 cup sugar
¾ teaspoon ground cinnamon
1 cup crushed cornflakes
1 egg white
1½ cups confectioners' sugar
2 tablespoons milk

✦ Preheat the oven to 400 degrees. Combine the flour and salt in a large bowl. Cut in the shortening and margarine with a pastry cutter until coarse crumbs form.

✦ Place the egg yolk in a measuring cup. Add enough milk to measure ⅔ cup. Pour into the flour mixture; mix well. Combine the apples, sugar and cinnamon in a bowl. Toss to coat the apples evenly with cinnamon sugar.

✦ Divide the dough into 2 equal portions. Pat 1 portion into the bottom of a jelly roll pan. Spread the cornflakes over the top. Arrange the apples over the cornflakes.

✦ Roll out the remaining dough between 2 sheets of waxed paper to equal the size of the pan. Peel off the top piece of paper and invert the dough, placing it on top of the apple mixture. Peel off the remaining paper.

✦ Beat the egg white in a small bowl until foamy. Brush the top of the dough with the egg white.

✦ Bake for 35 minutes or until golden. Let stand until cool. Combine the confectioners' sugar and 2 tablespoons milk in a small bowl; mix until smooth. Spread on the cooled pastry.

✦ Yield: 18 servings

Strawberry Pizza

1 cup flour

¼ cup confectioners' sugar

½ cup margarine, softened

1 cup mashed strawberries

¼ cup sugar

1 tablespoon cornstarch

½ teaspoon red food coloring

8 ounces cream cheese, softened

½ teaspoon vanilla extract

½ cup sugar

¼ teaspoon lemon juice

3 cups sliced strawberries

✦ Preheat the oven to 325 degrees. Combine the flour, confectioners' sugar and margarine in a mixer bowl. Beat at medium speed until well mixed.

✦ Pat the dough into a pizza pan. Bake for 15 minutes or until golden brown. Remove from the oven and cool completely.

✦ Combine the mashed strawberries and ¼ cup sugar in a saucepan. Dissolve the cornstarch in a small amount of water; add to the strawberry mixture. Cook over medium heat until the mixture thickens, stirring constantly. Add the food coloring; mix well. Remove from the heat and cool completely.

✦ Combine the cream cheese, vanilla, ½ cup sugar and lemon juice in a mixer bowl. Beat until light and fluffy. Spread mixture over the cooled crust. Arrange the sliced strawberries over the cream cheese mixture.

✦ Spread the strawberry sauce over the sliced strawberries. Chill for 2 hours.

✦ Yield: 8 servings

Mike Mickle
KWQC-TV6 Anchor

Mushroom Quiche

3 tablespoons margarine
1¼ pounds mushrooms, sliced
3 green onions, minced
1 clove of garlic, minced
3 shallots, minced
1¾ teaspoons dried oregano
1¾ teaspoons dried basil
1¼ teaspoons salt
¾ teaspoon dried marjoram
¼ teaspoon pepper
¼ teaspoon dried thyme
½ teaspoon dry mustard
4 eggs
¾ cup milk
1 unbaked (9-inch) pie shell

✦ Preheat the oven to 375 degrees. Melt the margarine in a large skillet over medium heat. Add the mushrooms, green onions, garlic and shallots. Sauté until the vegetables are soft.

✦ Add the oregano, basil, salt, marjoram, pepper, thyme and mustard. Cook for 2 minutes or until the liquid has evaporated, stirring occasionally. Remove from the heat. Let stand for 5 minutes.

✦ Beat the eggs and milk in a bowl until well combined. Stir in the mushroom mixture.

✦ Pour the mixture into the pie shell. Bake for 35 to 45 minutes or until the filling is puffed and the crust is beginning to brown.

✦ Yield: 6 servings

Mrs. George Bush
Wife of President George Bush

Chicken Strata

1 cup sliced water chestnuts, drained

¼ cup margarine

8 slices white bread, crusts removed

2 cups chopped cooked chicken or ham

8 ounces mushrooms, sliced

¼ cup margarine

8 slices processed cheese

4 eggs, beaten

¼ cup mayonnaise

2 cups milk

1 teaspoon salt

¼ cup chopped pimentos

1 (10-ounce) can cream of celery soup

1 cup cream of mushroom soup

Bread crumbs for topping

✦ Sauté the water chestnuts in ¼ cup margarine in a skillet. Arrange the bread in the bottom of a 9x13-inch baking pan. Cover with a layer of chicken, water chestnuts and mushrooms. Dot with ¼ cup margarine. Arrange the cheese slices over the mushrooms.

✦ Beat the eggs, mayonnaise, milk, salt, pimentos, celery soup and mushroom soup in a mixer bowl until well mixed. Pour over the cheese. Top with a layer of bread crumbs. Chill, covered, for 12 hours.

✦ Preheat the oven to 350 degrees. Bake, uncovered, for 1½ hours or until bubbly.

✦ Yield: 8 servings

Charles King
KWQC-TV6 Anchor

Sausage Soufflé

1½ pounds link sausage

8 slices white bread, cubed

2 cups shredded sharp Cheddar cheese

2½ cups milk

4 eggs

2¼ teaspoons dry mustard

1 (10-ounce) can cream of mushroom soup

½ cup milk

✦ Brown the sausage in a skillet; drain well. Cut into bite-size pieces.

✦ Arrange the bread cubes in the bottom of a greased 9x13-inch baking pan. Sprinkle the cheese and sausage over the top.

✦ Combine 2½ cups milk, eggs and mustard in a bowl; mix well. Pour over the cheese mixture. Chill, covered, for 12 hours.

✦ Preheat the oven to 350 degrees. Remove the soufflé from the refrigerator and uncover.

✦ Combine the soup and ½ cup milk in a bowl; mix well. Pour over the top of the soufflé. Bake for 1½ hours or until puffed and brown.

✦ Yield: 10 servings

Tom and Jerry

12 egg whites

⅛ teaspoon cream of tartar

1 (16-ounce) package confectioners' sugar

12 egg yolks

⅛ teaspoon ground cinnamon

Dash of allspice

⅛ teaspoon grated nutmeg

3 ounces rum

9 cups boiling water

18 ounces rum

6 ounces brandy

✦ Beat the egg whites and cream of tartar in a mixer bowl until soft peaks form. Add the confectioners' sugar gradually, beating constantly until stiff peaks form.

✦ Beat the egg yolks in a separate mixer bowl until thick. Fold in the egg whites. Fold in the cinnamon, allspice, nutmeg and 3 ounces rum.

✦ Heat 12 mugs with boiling water or in a steamer.

✦ Place ¼ cup of the egg mixture in the bottom of each mug. Add ¾ cup boiling water, 1½ ounces rum and ½ ounce brandy to each mug. Fill the mug with additional boiling water if needed. Garnish each serving with grated nutmeg.

✦ Yield: 12 servings

Jim Graham
KWQC-TV6 Vice President and General Manager

Beef & Pork

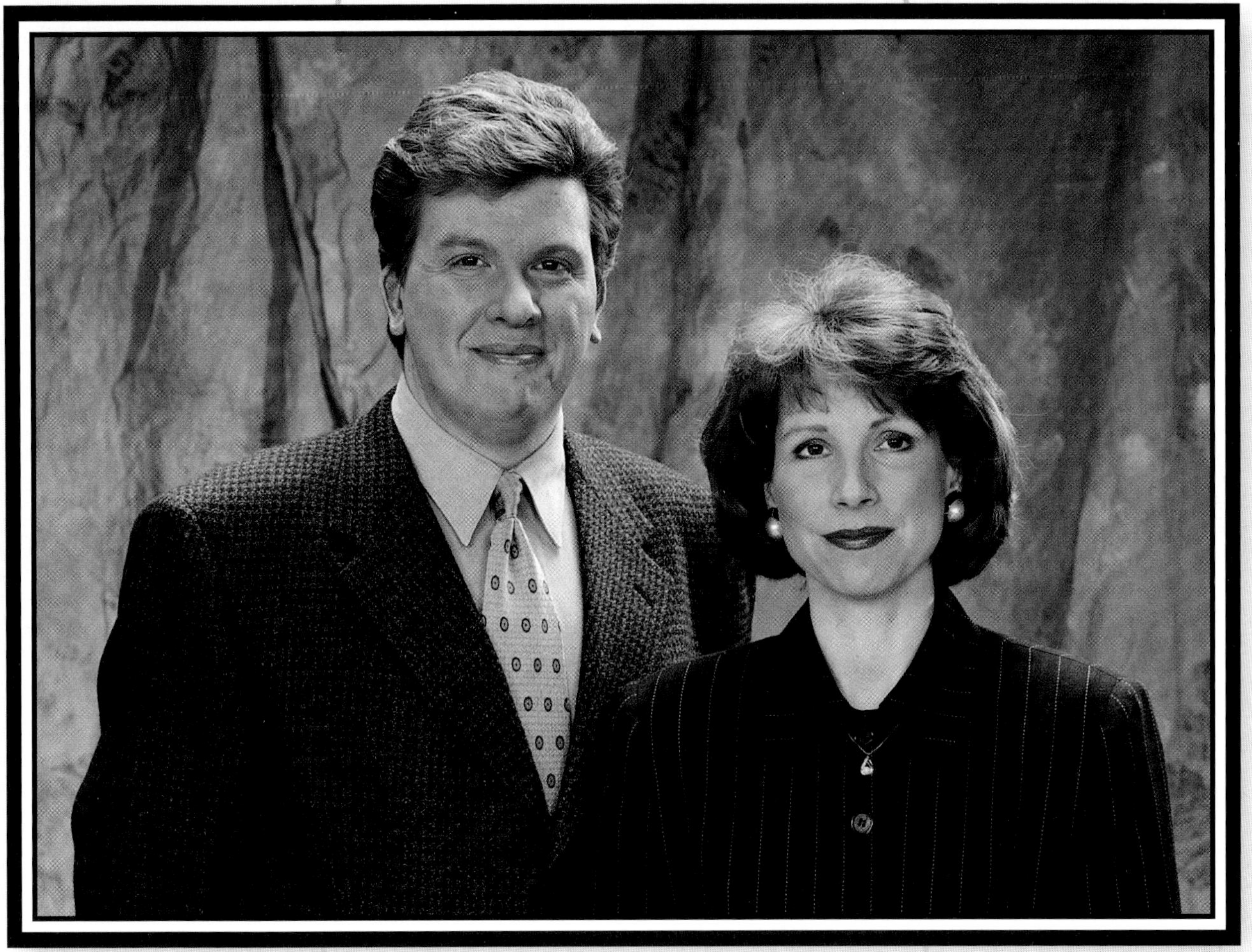

Mike Mickle

Marcia Lense

The American Red Cross, Quad Cities Chapter, is made up of caring volunteers who are standing by around the clock to assist local families through crises and disasters. The Red Cross also provides education services such as first aid and CPR training, disaster preparedness training, and HIV/AIDS education. The American Red Cross is the only voluntary organization chartered by Congress to provide special services to disaster victims.

KWQC-TV6

The Quad City Times Bix 7 is a 7-mile out-and-back race that draws 20,000 walkers and runners to Brady Street Hill. The race is broadcast live on KWQC-TV6 and is beamed around the world on the Armed Forces Network. The annual race is part of the Bix Beiderbecke weekend celebration that includes a street festival and the Bix Jazz Festival.

Photo Courtesy of the Quad City Times

KWQC-TV6

Beef & Pork

Italian Beef

1 (4- to 5-pound) beef roast
3 to 4 cups water
1 envelope onion soup mix
2 tablespoons basil
2 tablespoons oregano
½ teaspoon crushed red pepper
¼ teaspoon garlic salt
1 teaspoon salt
½ teaspoon black pepper

✦ Place the roast in a slow cooker. Combine the water, soup mix, basil, oregano, red pepper, garlic salt, salt and black pepper in a saucepan. Bring to a boil over high heat. Pour over the roast.

✦ Cook on Low for 6 to 8 hours or until the roast is tender and cooked through. Serve thinly sliced roast on deli rolls with the juice served on the side.

✦ Yield: 6 to 8 servings

Chop Suey Bake

1 pound ground beef
1 small onion, chopped
1 cup chopped celery
1 (10-ounce) can cream of chicken soup
1 (10-ounce) can cream of mushroom soup
1 cup water
½ cup instant rice
3 tablespoons soy sauce
1 (3-ounce) can chow mein noodles

✦ Preheat the oven to 350 degrees. Brown the ground beef in a skillet, stirring until crumbly; drain well. Add the onion, celery, chicken soup, mushroom soup and water; mix well. Stir in the rice and soy sauce.

✦ Transfer the mixture to a 9x13-inch baking pan. Bake, covered, for 30 minutes. Remove from the oven, uncover, and sprinkle the noodles over the top. Bake, uncovered, for 30 minutes or until bubbly and heated through.

✦ Yield: 4 servings

Ed Zack
Former WOC Sports Anchor

On October 31, 1949, when WOC (now KWQC-TV6) signed on the air, there were 400 homes in the Quad Cities that had television sets. One week later, 1,750 homes had sets; less than two months later, 5,039 homes did. By June 1950, there were more than 11,000 sets in the Quad Cities; in December 1950, there were 40,000 sets in Scott and Rock Island counties. Today, 303,810 households in the KWQC-TV6 viewing area have sets.

Cottage Pie

¼ cup butter

1 cup chopped onion

1½ pounds lean ground beef

Salt and pepper to taste

¼ teaspoon ground savory

1 cup prepared brown gravy

2 cups mashed cooked potatoes

2 tablespoons butter

✦ Preheat the oven to 400 degrees. Melt ¼ cup butter in a medium skillet. Add the onion. Sauté until lightly browned. Add the ground beef, salt, pepper and savory; mix well. Cook for 5 minutes or until the ground beef is brown and crumbly. Stir in the gravy. Cook until bubbly.

✦ Transfer the mixture to a buttered 8-cup casserole. Arrange the mashed potatoes on top of the ground beef mixture. Dot with 2 tablespoons butter. Bake for 30 minutes.

✦ Yield: 4 servings

Taco Casserole

1 pound ground beef

1 small onion, chopped

1 (15-ounce) can tomato sauce

1 envelope taco seasoning mix

½ tomato sauce can water

1 (8-ounce) package tortilla chips

2 cups shredded Cheddar cheese

✦ Preheat the oven to 350 degrees. Brown the ground beef with the onion in a skillet, stirring until the ground beef is crumbly; drain well. Stir in the tomato sauce, taco seasoning mix and water. Simmer for 5 minutes.

✦ Crush the tortilla chips and place in the bottom of a 4-quart casserole. Spread the ground beef mixture over the chips. Sprinkle the cheese evenly across the top. Bake for 10 minutes or until the cheese is melted.

✦ Yield: 6 servings

What's-in-the-Cupboard Goulash

12 ounces ground beef

1/3 cup chopped onion

3 cups warm water

1 (7 1/2-ounce) package macaroni and cheese

1 (14-ounce) can stewed tomatoes

Pinch of garlic powder

Salt and pepper to taste

✦ Brown the ground beef with the onion in a large skillet, stirring until the ground beef is crumbly; drain well.

✦ Add the water and macaroni to the ground beef, reserving the packet of dry cheese. Cook for 10 minutes or until the macaroni is tender, stirring occasionally.

✦ Stir in the dry cheese, stewed tomatoes, garlic powder, salt and pepper. Cook until the mixture is thick and heated through, stirring occasionally.

✦ Serve garnished with shredded Cheddar cheese, if desired.

✦ Yield: 3 to 4 servings

Charles King, currently anchor of "Quad Cities Today" on KWQC-TV6, has been a part of the station for many years, working in both radio and television.

Beefy Mac Goulash

1 pound ground beef or ground venison

½ medium onion, chopped

½ cup chopped mushrooms (optional)

½ cup chopped green bell pepper

1 (28-ounce) can peeled tomatoes, chopped

1 (10-ounce) can tomato soup

2 tablespoons chili powder

¼ cup catsup

Salt and pepper to taste

1 (12-ounce) package shell macaroni

✦ Brown the ground beef with the onion, mushrooms and green pepper in a skillet, stirring until the ground beef is crumbly; drain well.

✦ Stir in the tomatoes, tomato soup, chili powder, catsup, salt and pepper. Simmer for 10 minutes.

✦ Cook the macaroni according to the package directions. Drain, but do not rinse.

✦ Add the macaroni to the ground beef mixture; mix well. Serve immediately.

✦ Yield: 4 servings

Artist and TV personality Ken Wagner entertained his viewers by drawing pictures.

Meaty Lasagna

1 pound ground beef

8 ounces mild sausage

1 (28-ounce) jar spaghetti sauce with mushrooms

24 ounces cottage cheese

9 lasagna noodles, cooked, drained

2 cups shredded mozzarella cheese

✦ Preheat the oven to 350 degrees. Brown the ground beef and sausage in a skillet, stirring until the ground beef and sausage are crumbly; drain well.

✦ Stir in the spaghetti sauce. Cook over medium heat until heated through.

✦ Drain any excess liquid from the cottage cheese. Layer the noodles, ground beef mixture, cottage cheese and mozzarella cheese ⅓ at a time in a large baking dish.

✦ Bake for 30 minutes or until the top is brown and bubbly. Cool slightly before cutting and serving.

✦ Yield: 8 to 10 servings

Fran Riley
KWQC-TV6 Anchor

Mom's Microwave Lasagna

1 pound ground beef

1 (32-ounce) jar spaghetti sauce

½ cup water

1 teaspoon garlic salt

1 teaspoon oregano

1 (8-ounce) package lasagna noodles

16 ounces ricotta cheese

3 cups shredded mozzarella cheese

✦ Brown the ground beef in a skillet, stirring until crumbly; drain well. Stir in the spaghetti sauce, water, garlic salt and oregano. Simmer for 15 minutes.

✦ Transfer ⅓ of the ground beef mixture to a 9x13-inch glass baking dish. Add layers of half the uncooked lasagna noodles, half the ricotta cheese and 1 cup of the mozzarella cheese. Continue layering with ½ of the remaining ground beef mixture, remaining lasagna noodles, remaining ricotta cheese and 1 cup of the mozzarella cheese. Top with the remaining ground beef mixture and mozzarella cheese.

✦ Wrap the baking dish with a double thickness of plastic wrap. Microwave on Medium for 30 minutes.

✦ *Note:* Before you begin to prepare this easy lasagna, make sure your glass baking dish fits in the microwave oven.

✦ Yield: 15 servings

Saucy Italian Meatballs

1 pound ground beef
8 ounces hot Italian sausage
½ cup bread crumbs
1 egg, lightly beaten
½ cup finely chopped onion
½ teaspoon salt
1 (10-ounce) can golden mushroom soup
¼ cup water
⅛ teaspoon garlic powder
¼ teaspoon dried oregano
6 hard rolls, split

✦ Combine the ground beef, sausage, bread crumbs, egg, onion and salt in a bowl; mix well.

✦ Shape the ground beef mixture into 24 meatballs.

✦ Cook the meatballs in a skillet over medium-high heat until cooked through; drain well.

✦ Combine the soup, water, garlic powder and oregano in a bowl; mix well. Pour over the meatballs. Simmer, covered, for 20 minutes.

✦ Spoon the meatballs and sauce over the split rolls.

✦ Yield: 6 servings

In 1960, Vern Gielow played the popular Cap'n Vern, pictured here with Tommy the puppet and Calliope the turtle.

Porcupine Meatballs

- 1 egg, beaten
- 1 (10-ounce) can tomato soup
- ¼ cup long grain rice
- ¼ teaspoon pepper
- ¼ teaspoon onion powder
- 1 pound lean ground beef
- ½ teaspoon dried oregano
- 1 teaspoon Worcestershire sauce
- ½ cup water

✦ Combine the egg, ¼ cup of the soup, rice, pepper and onion powder in a bowl; mix well. Add the ground beef; mix thoroughly.

✦ Shape the ground beef mixture into 20 meatballs. Place the meatballs in a large skillet.

✦ Combine the remaining soup, oregano, Worcestershire sauce and water in a bowl. Pour over the meatballs.

✦ Bring to a boil over high heat. Reduce the heat. Simmer, covered, for 20 minutes or until the ground beef is cooked through, stirring occasionally. Skim and discard any fat. Serve immediately.

✦ Yield: 4 to 5 servings

Jack Thomsen anchored the evening news from the studios of WOC.

Sweet-and-Sour Meatballs

1½ pounds ground beef
¾ cup rolled oats
1 cup tomato sauce
1 teaspoon salt
½ teaspoon pepper
1 tablespoon chopped onion
3 tablespoons sugar
3 tablespoons vinegar
½ cup water
1 cup catsup

✦ Preheat the oven to 350 degrees. Combine the ground beef, oats, tomato sauce, salt, pepper and onion in a bowl; mix well.

✦ Shape the ground beef into 1-inch meatballs. Place the meatballs in a single layer in a 9x13-inch baking pan.

✦ Combine the sugar, vinegar, water and catsup in a bowl; mix well. Pour over the meatballs.

✦ Bake for 1 hour, turning the meatballs after 30 minutes.

✦ Yield: 4 to 6 servings

Operations were moved from the old Ryan building to the new building in 1963. The Ryan residence was leveled shortly thereafter, but the exterior of the annex was resurfaced in brick to match the new building.

Slow-Cooker Enchiladas

1 pound ground beef
1 cup chopped onion
½ cup chopped green bell pepper
1 (15-ounce) can pinto beans or kidney beans, drained, rinsed
1 (15-ounce) can black beans, drained, rinsed
1 (10-ounce) can tomatoes with green chiles
⅓ cup water
1 teaspoon chili powder
½ teaspoon ground cumin
½ teaspoon salt
¼ teaspoon pepper
1 cup shredded Cheddar cheese
1 cup shredded Monterey Jack cheese
6 flour tortillas

✦ Brown the ground beef with the onion and green pepper in a skillet, stirring until the ground beef is crumbly; drain well.

✦ Add the pinto beans, black beans, tomatoes with green chiles, water, chili powder, cumin, salt and pepper; mix well. Bring to a boil. Reduce the heat. Simmer, covered, for 10 minutes.

✦ Toss the Cheddar cheese and Monterey Jack cheese in a bowl with a fork. Layer ¾ cup of the ground beef mixture, 1 tortilla and ⅓ cup of the cheese mixture in a 5-quart slow cooker.

✦ Continue layering with the remaining ingredients until all the ingredients are used, ending with the cheese mixture. Cook, covered, on Low for 5 to 7 hours.

✦ Yield: 4 servings

Stuffed Green Peppers

6 green bell peppers
1½ pounds ground beef
1 medium onion, finely chopped
1 tablespoon chili powder
2 eggs, beaten
1 cup catsup
1 cup crushed cornflakes
Salt and pepper to taste
1½ cups catsup
1 cup tomato paste
2 tablespoons brown sugar
2 tablespoons dry mustard
1 tablespoon vinegar

✦ Preheat the oven to 375 degrees. Remove the stems and cut the green peppers into halves vertically. Remove and discard the seeds.

✦ Boil the peppers in water to cover in a saucepan for 5 minutes; drain. Set aside.

✦ Combine the ground beef, onion, chili powder, eggs, catsup, cornflakes, salt and pepper in a bowl; mix thoroughly. Stuff each pepper half with the ground beef mixture. Arrange cut side up in a glass baking dish.

✦ For the sauce, combine the catsup, tomato paste, brown sugar, mustard and vinegar in a bowl; mix well. Pour over the stuffed peppers.

✦ Bake for 30 to 40 minutes or until the ground beef is cooked through.

✦ Yield: 6 servings

Mrs. Richard Petty
Wife of Race Car Driver Richard Petty

Barbecue Sandwiches

12 ounces ground beef
1 small onion, chopped
1 (14-ounce) bottle catsup
2 tablespoons flour
1 cup water
½ cup packed light brown sugar
1 (12-ounce) can corned beef, shredded
Chili powder to taste
4 sandwich rolls

✦ Brown the ground beef in a skillet, stirring until crumbly; drain well. Stir in the onion and catsup.

✦ Sprinkle the flour over the ground beef mixture; stir to combine. Stir in the water, brown sugar, corned beef and chili powder.

✦ Simmer for 1 hour, stirring occasionally. Spoon over split sandwich rolls. Serve immediately.

✦ Yield: 4 servings

Dateline October 18, 1949—WOC News studios are located in one of Davenport's oldest landmarks. In 1870, the building housed a girls' school; later it was occupied by the Ed Ryan family. The interior of the structure has been remodeled to contain all the radio and television operations of the station. The exterior remains residential in appearance, making it unique among Davenport business establishments.

Hickory-Smoked Leg of Lamb

1 (4- to 6-pound) leg of lamb

3 cloves of garlic, sliced, or to taste

3 (8-ounce) cans limeade

½ teaspoon crushed rosemary, or to taste

½ cup white wine vinegar

✦ Make small slits in the lamb using a sharp paring knife. Insert a slice of garlic in each slit.

✦ Combine the limeade, rosemary and vinegar in a large bowl. Add the lamb, turning to coat with the marinade. Marinate in the refrigerator for 12 hours, turning occasionally.

✦ Preheat a smoker or outdoor grill. Soak chunks of hickory in water for 30 minutes. Remove the lamb from the marinade and pat dry. Discard the marinade. Sear the lamb over hot coals until browned on all sides. Remove the lamb from the grill. Rearrange the coals to accommodate a pan of water in the middle. Add hickory chunks on top of the coals. Replace the rack and position the lamb over the bowl of water; cover the grill.

✦ Grill for 3 hours or until a meat thermometer inserted in the thickest part of the lamb reads 160 degrees for medium. Add more hickory chunks as needed.

✦ Yield: 6 to 8 servings

Bourbon Cashew-Studded Ham

1½ cups herb-seasoned stuffing mix

½ cup melted butter

3 tablespoons prepared mustard

3 eggs, beaten

¾ cup chopped parsley

1 cup bourbon

1 cup packed light brown sugar

¼ teaspoon ground cloves

1 (5- to 6-pound) cooked ham

12 to 20 whole cashews

✦ For the stuffing, combine the stuffing mix, butter, mustard, eggs and parsley in a bowl; mix well.

✦ For the sauce, combine the bourbon, brown sugar and cloves in a saucepan. Simmer over medium-high heat for 5 minutes.

✦ Place the ham in a 9x13-inch baking dish. Use an apple corer to make 6 to 10 holes at 2-inch intervals in the top of the ham. Insert 1 cashew in each hole, followed by a spoonful of stuffing and a second cashew. Pour the bourbon sauce over the ham after all the holes are filled.

✦ Bake, uncovered, for 1½ hours or until the crust is golden brown, basting with bourbon sauce every 20 minutes.

✦ Yield: 20 to 25 servings

Rick Benjamin
Former KWQC-TV6 Anchor

Hearty Meatballs

1 pound ground beef
1 pound ground ham
1 pound ground pork
1 teaspoon salt
1½ cups milk
2 cups graham cracker crumbs
2 eggs, beaten
1 cup packed brown sugar
1 cup tomato soup concentrate
¼ cup vinegar
1½ tablespoons prepared mustard
¼ teaspoon Worcestershire sauce

✦ Combine the ground beef, ham, ground pork, salt, milk, graham cracker crumbs and eggs in a large bowl; mix thoroughly. Chill, covered, for 2 to 3 hours.

✦ Preheat the oven to 325 degrees. Remove the meat mixture from the refrigerator. Shape into meatballs and arrange in the bottom of a baking dish.

✦ Whisk the brown sugar, tomato soup concentrate, vinegar, mustard and Worcestershire sauce together in a bowl. Pour over the meatballs.

✦ Bake, covered with foil, for 1 hour or until the meatballs are cooked through.

✦ Yield: 8 to 12 servings

Ernie Mimms (Captain Ernie) and Paula Sands.

Pork Chops with Beer and Pears

6 loin pork chops
½ teaspoon salt
½ teaspoon pepper
1 tablespoon butter
1 large onion, sliced into strips or rings
2 teaspoons sugar
¾ cup beer or apple juice
½ cup water
1 (16-ounce) can pear halves, drained

✦ Trim and discard the fat from the pork chops. Sprinkle salt and pepper over the pork chops.

✦ Melt the butter in a 12-inch skillet over medium heat. Add the onion. Sauté until tender. Remove the onion and set aside.

✦ Add the pork chops to the skillet and brown well on both sides. Add the sautéed onion.

✦ Combine the sugar, beer and water in a bowl. Pour over the pork chops. Simmer for 10 minutes or until the beer turns golden brown.

✦ Place the pear halves on top of the pork chops. Simmer, covered, for 20 minutes or until the pork chops are cooked through.

✦ Remove the cover. Simmer for 5 minutes, basting the pears occasionally with the pan drippings.

✦ Yield: 6 servings

Orange and Ginger-Glazed Pork Roast

1 (3- to 4-pound) boneless pork loin

2 tablespoons vegetable oil

2 teaspoons dried thyme

1 teaspoon ground sage

2 teaspoons salt

1 teaspoon freshly ground pepper

¼ teaspoon ground allspice

2 cloves of garlic, minced

½ cup orange marmalade

⅓ cup Dijon mustard

1 tablespoon grated fresh ginger

1 tablespoon Worcestershire sauce

¼ teaspoon salt

¼ teaspoon freshly ground pepper

✦ Rub the pork with the vegetable oil; set aside. For the dry marinade, combine the thyme, sage, 2 teaspoons salt, 1 teaspoon pepper, allspice and garlic in a bowl; mix well. Coat the pork evenly with the dry marinade. Marinate in the refrigerator for 1 hour. For the liquid marinade, combine the marmalade, Dijon mustard, ginger, Worcestershire sauce, ¼ teaspoon salt and ¼ teaspoon pepper in a bowl; mix well.

✦ Prepare a fire for indirect cooking in a covered outdoor grill. Oil the rack and position it 4 to 6 inches above the fire. Place the pork on the rack but not directly over the fire; cover the grill and open the vents halfway. Cook for 45 minutes. Turn the pork. Cook for 45 minutes longer or until a meat thermometer registers 160 degrees, basting with the liquid marinade every 10 minutes and turning the pork once or twice.

✦ Remove the pork from the grill. Let stand, covered with foil, for 10 minutes. Carve and serve.

✦ Yield: 6 to 8 servings

Sheldon Ripson
Former WOC Anchor

Paula Sand

To Bernice - Love,
Paula

KWQC-TV6

Carne de Puerco

1 pound tomatillos

6 jalapeños

1 (4-pound) boneless pork loin

1 tablespoon vegetable oil

2 (14-ounce) cans diced tomatoes

1 teaspoon ground cumin

Salt to taste

✦ Remove the papery skins from the tomatillos. Remove the stems and seeds from the jalapeños. Place the tomatillos and jalapeños in a medium saucepan; cover with hot water. Boil for 10 minutes or until the tomatillos are soft. Remove from the heat; set aside to cool.

✦ Trim and discard any fat or gristle from the pork. Cut the pork into 1-inch cubes.

✦ Heat the vegetable oil in a large skillet over medium-high heat. Add the pork. Cook until lightly browned and cooked through.

✦ Transfer the pork to a large saucepan. Strain the cooled tomatillo mixture, reserving 1 cup of the liquid.

✦ Place the tomatillos and jalapeños in a blender container. Process with the reserved liquid. Add the tomatoes, cumin and salt. Process until smooth.

✦ Pour the tomatillo mixture over the pork. Heat until warmed through, stirring occasionally. Serve immediately.

✦ Yield: 10 to 12 servings

Paula Sands
KWQC-TV6 Anchor and Host of
"Paula Sands Live"

Mostaccioli Marinara

6 Italian sausages, mild or hot

8 ounces mostaccioli or other tubular pasta

1 (25-ounce) jar marinara sauce

3 Roma tomatoes, seeded and diced

3 cups shredded mozzarella cheese

1 tablespoon chopped fresh basil, or 1 teaspoon dried

1 tablespoon chopped fresh oregano, or 1 teaspoon dried

✦ Preheat the oven to 400 degrees. Cook the sausages in a skillet until browned and cooked through; drain well on paper towels.

✦ Cook the mostaccioli according to the package directions; drain and set aside.

✦ Pour half the marinara sauce into a 4-inch-deep, 8x8-inch flame-proof casserole. Place the casserole over medium heat. Add enough mostaccioli to half fill the casserole. Stir to coat the pasta with the sauce.

✦ Cut the sausages into ½-inch slices; add to the casserole. Stir in the tomatoes and remaining marinara sauce. Add the remaining pasta; mix well. Add half the cheese to the corners and middle of the casserole. Cook for 2 minutes. Stir to mix well.

✦ Sprinkle the basil and oregano over the top. Simmer for 15 minutes, stirring occasionally. Sprinkle the remaining cheese over the top; cover.

✦ Bake for 15 minutes. Remove from the oven and let stand for 10 minutes before serving.

✦ Yield: 3 to 5 servings

Erik Maitland
KWQC-TV6 Weather Anchor

Italian Broccoli Spaghetti

- 4 quarts water
- 1 (16-ounce) package spaghetti
- ½ (10-ounce) package frozen cut broccoli
- 12 ounces Italian sausage, cut into ½-inch pieces
- 2 tablespoons olive oil
- 2 tablespoons melted butter
- ¼ teaspoon garlic powder
- Salt and pepper to taste
- ¾ cup grated Parmesan cheese

✦ Bring the water to a boil in a large stockpot. Add the spaghetti. Cook for 2 minutes. Add the broccoli. Cook for 8 minutes.

✦ Brown the sausage in a large skillet over medium-high heat until cooked through; drain well. Return the sausage to the skillet and add a mixture of the olive oil, butter and garlic powder.

✦ Drain the spaghetti and broccoli. Add to the sausage. Add the salt, pepper and cheese; mix well. Serve immediately.

✦ Yield: 6 servings

Photographer Hash

- 2 tablespoons vegetable oil or bacon drippings
- 1 medium onion, sliced
- 12 ounces smoked sausage, cut into ½-inch pieces
- ¼ cup vinegar
- 2 teaspoons prepared horseradish
- ½ teaspoon sugar
- ½ teaspoon caraway seeds, ground
- 1½ cups cooked cubed potatoes
- 2 to 3 cups shredded cabbage
- Salt to taste

✦ Heat the oil in a skillet over medium-high heat. Add the onion. Cook until translucent.

✦ Add the sausage. Cook until the sausage is brown and cooked through.

✦ Add the vinegar, horseradish, sugar and caraway seeds. Cook for 5 minutes, stirring occasionally.

✦ Add the potatoes and cabbage; mix well. Cook until the cabbage is tender-crisp, stirring occasionally. Season with salt. Serve immediately.

✦ Yield: 4 servings

Poultry & Seafood

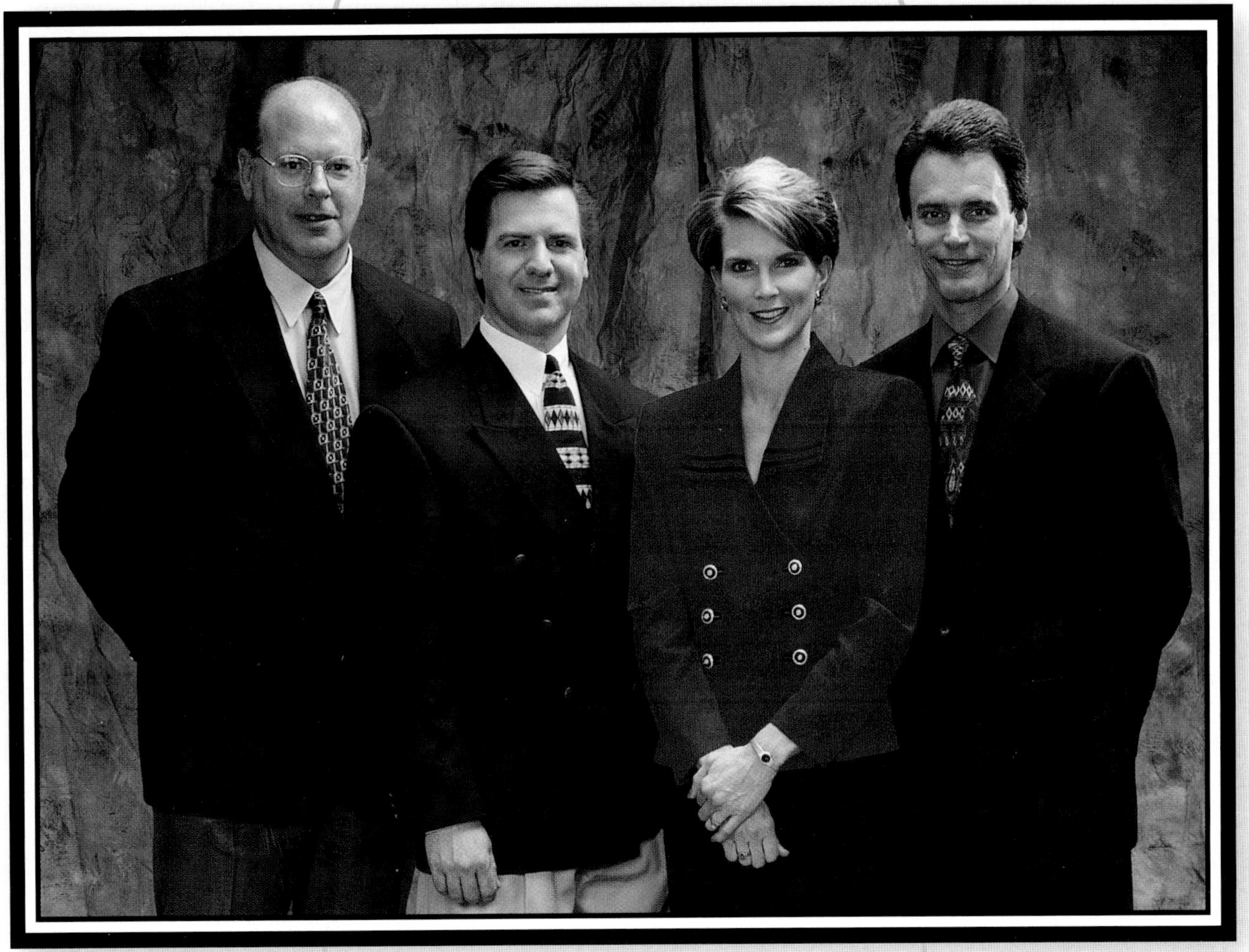

Thom Cornelis

Gary Metivier

Sharon DeRycke

Terry Swails

Each November the glow from the Festival of Trees radiates throughout the region as thousands walk through the winter wonderland of trees, wreaths, stockings, and gingerbread houses. Quad City Arts hosts the Festival of Trees to raise money and awareness for local arts.

KWQC-TV6

A special part of the Festival of Trees is the holiday parade . . . an annual tradition of balloons, children, music, and laughter. On parade day the streets of downtown Davenport sport their holiday best and are packed with thousands of spectators of all ages. The holiday spirit arrives as you hear the marching bands, watch for Santa, and see the children's faces as the huge, helium-filled characters float down the street. KWQC-TV6 broadcasts the parade live each year so that thousands can enjoy this wonderful holiday tradition.

KWQC-TV6

Poultry & Seafood

Chicken Alexandria

½ onion, chopped
2 cups chopped cooked chicken breast
1 (8-ounce) package spaghetti, cooked
1 (10-ounce) can cream of mushroom soup
2 tablespoons dry sherry
⅓ cup chopped toasted almonds
1 teaspoon minced parsley
1 cup sour cream
½ cup buttered bread crumbs

✦ Preheat the oven to 350 degrees. Sauté the onion briefly in a nonstick skillet.

✦ Combine the chicken, spaghetti, soup, onion, sherry, almonds, parsley and sour cream in a bowl; mix well.

✦ Transfer the chicken mixture to a greased 9x13-inch baking dish. Scatter the bread crumbs over the top. Bake for 35 minutes or until brown and bubbly.

✦ Yield: 4 to 6 servings

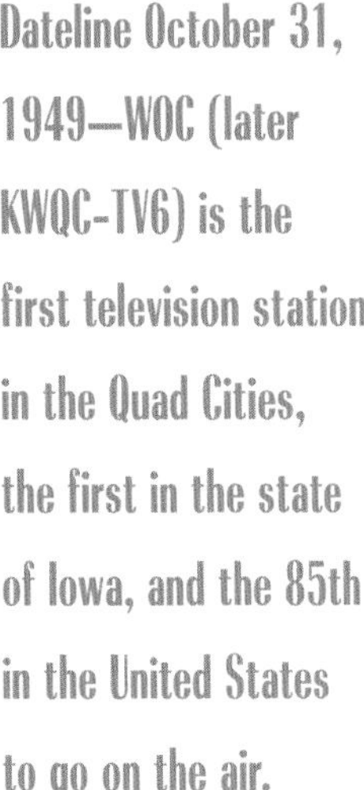
Dateline October 31, 1949—WOC (later KWQC-TV6) is the first television station in the Quad Cities, the first in the state of Iowa, and the 85th in the United States to go on the air.

Through the years the station has had many dedicated employees, including several spouses and children who have worked together at the station. Three generations of the Zack family have been employed at the station.

Chicken Cantonese

4 boneless skinless chicken breasts

¼ cup vegetable oil

1 cup slivered almonds

½ teaspoon salt

1½ cups chopped celery

1 cup sliced Spanish onion

½ cup chicken broth

1 teaspoon sugar

1¼ tablespoons cornstarch

¼ cup soy sauce

1 cup chicken broth

1 (5-ounce) can bamboo shoots, drained

1 (5-ounce) can water chestnuts, drained

3 cups hot cooked rice

✦ Slice the chicken into thin strips; set aside. Heat the oil in a large skillet over medium-high heat. Add the almonds. Cook until brown, stirring constantly. Remove the almonds with a slotted spoon; drain on paper towels.

✦ Sprinkle the chicken with salt. Place in the skillet. Sauté for 5 to 10 minutes or until tender and cooked through. Remove the chicken; set aside.

✦ Add the celery, onion and ½ cup chicken broth to the skillet. Cook for 5 minutes or until the vegetables are tender-crisp.

✦ Combine the sugar, cornstarch, soy sauce and 1 cup chicken broth in a small bowl; mix well. Pour over the celery mixture. Cook until the sauce thickens, stirring constantly.

✦ Add the chicken, almonds, bamboo shoots and water chestnuts and heat thoroughly. Serve over hot rice.

✦ Yield: 4 to 6 servings

Hal Hart
Former WOC Sports Anchor

Grilled Orange Chicken

½ cup olive oil

2 teaspoons minced fresh garlic, or to taste

1 teaspoon freshly ground pepper, or to taste

2 teaspoons chopped fresh rosemary, or to taste

4 boneless chicken breasts

½ cup freshly squeezed orange juice

½ to 1 teaspoon orange zest

✦ Combine the olive oil, garlic, pepper and rosemary in a sealable plastic bag; mix well. Add the chicken and turn the bag to coat the chicken with the marinade. Seal the bag. Marinate in the refrigerator for 12 hours.

✦ Add the orange juice and orange zest to the marinade. Turn to mix and coat the chicken well. Return the chicken to the refrigerator. Marinate for 4 hours.

✦ Preheat the grill. Drain the chicken, discarding the marinade. Place the chicken on the grill rack over hot coals. Cover the grill immediately to extinguish any flare-ups.

✦ Grill for 2 to 3 minutes per side or until the chicken is cooked through, turning once. Serve over a bed of freshly sautéed spinach.

✦ Yield: 4 servings

Leeza Gibbons
Host of "Leeza"

Sharon DeRycke

Chicken Oregano Sauté

2 tablespoons chopped fresh oregano, or 2 teaspoons dried

¾ teaspoon salt

¼ teaspoon pepper

1 pound boneless skinless chicken breasts

1 tablespoon olive oil

1 clove of garlic, thinly sliced

2 tablespoons olive oil

1 pound small red potatoes, thinly sliced

1 pint cherry tomatoes, cut into halves

4 ounces fresh spinach

1 bunch fresh arugula

½ cup crumbled feta cheese

✦ Combine the oregano, salt and pepper in a small bowl; mix well. Cut the chicken into thin strips. Sprinkle half the oregano mixture over the chicken.

✦ Heat 1 tablespoon olive oil in a skillet over medium-high heat. Add the garlic. Cook for 3 minutes or until golden brown, stirring constantly. Remove the garlic and set aside.

✦ Add the chicken to the skillet. Cook for 5 minutes or until cooked through, stirring constantly. Transfer the chicken to a plate; keep warm.

✦ Add 2 tablespoons olive oil to the skillet. Reduce the heat to medium. Add the potatoes. Cook, covered, for 10 minutes or until the potatoes are tender, stirring occasionally.

✦ Add the tomatoes, spinach, arugula, chicken and remaining oregano mixture. Cook for 3 minutes or until the greens are wilted and the chicken is heated through, stirring occasionally.

✦ Stir in the garlic. Sprinkle with feta cheese. Serve immediately.

✦ Yield: 6 servings

Sharon DeRycke
KWQC-TV6 Anchor

Chicken and Potato Bake

1 tablespoon vegetable oil

4 boneless skinless chicken breasts

1 (10-ounce) can cream of celery soup

½ cup milk

½ cup sour cream

½ teaspoon seasoned salt

¼ teaspoon pepper

1 (24-ounce) package Potatoes O'Brien, thawed

1 cup shredded Cheddar cheese

1 (3-ounce) can French-fried onions

✦ Preheat the oven to 350 degrees. Heat the oil in a large skillet over medium-high heat. Add the chicken. Cook for 10 minutes or until brown, turning occasionally.

✦ Combine the soup, milk, sour cream, seasoned salt and pepper in a large bowl; mix well. Stir in the potatoes, ½ cup of the cheese and ½ can of the onions. Spoon the mixture into a 9x13-inch baking dish.

✦ Arrange the chicken over the potato mixture.

✦ Bake, covered with foil, for 40 minutes or until bubbly. Remove the foil. Sprinkle the remaining cheese and remaining onions over the top. Bake for 5 minutes or until the cheese is melted.

✦ Yield: 4 servings

Chicken and Corn Bread Casserole

4 skinless chicken breasts

½ cup melted margarine

1 (6-ounce) package corn bread stuffing mix

1 cup sour cream

1 (10-ounce) can cream of chicken soup

1½ to 2 cups chicken broth

✦ Preheat the oven to 350 degrees. Poach the chicken in simmering water in a skillet for 45 minutes or until cooked through. Let cool.

✦ Remove the chicken from the bone. Cut into bite-size pieces.

✦ Pour the margarine into a medium casserole. Layer ¾ of the stuffing mix and accompanying seasonings over the margarine. Arrange the chicken over the stuffing.

✦ Combine the sour cream, soup and 1 cup of the chicken broth in a bowl; mix well. Spoon over the chicken. Layer the remaining stuffing mix over the sour cream mixture.

✦ Pour enough of the remaining chicken broth over the stuffing mix to moisten. Bake for 45 to 60 minutes or until heated through.

✦ Yield: 6 to 8 servings

Make-Ahead Chicken Casserole

1 (7-ounce) package elbow macaroni

2 cups milk

1 (10-ounce) can cream of mushroom soup

2 cups shredded Cheddar cheese

2 cups chopped cooked chicken

½ teaspoon salt

1 envelope onion soup mix

✦ Combine the macaroni, milk, mushroom soup, cheese, chicken, salt and onion soup mix in a large bowl; mix well. Chill, covered, for 8 to 12 hours.

✦ Preheat the oven to 350 degrees. Coat an 8x10-inch baking pan with nonstick cooking spray.

✦ Pour the macaroni mixture into the prepared pan. Bake for 1 hour or until bubbly and heated through.

✦ Yield: 4 to 6 servings

WOC anchors Paula Sands and Don Rhyne in the mid-1980s.

Mexican Pasta

12 ounces penne or macaroni

2 cups shredded cooked chicken

1 cup salsa

3/4 cup frozen corn kernels

1 cup shredded Cheddar cheese

✦ Cook the pasta according to the package directions; drain and set aside.

✦ Combine the chicken, salsa and corn in a skillet. Cook over medium heat until heated through, stirring occasionally.

✦ Add 3/4 cup of the cheese to the chicken mixture; mix well. Add the pasta when the cheese begins to melt.

✦ Cook until the pasta is heated through, stirring frequently.

✦ Serve with the remaining cheese sprinkled over each serving.

✦ Yield: 4 servings

KWQC-TV6

Gary Metivier

Sizzlin' Chicken Stir-Fry

2 tablespoons vegetable oil

1½ pounds boneless skinless chicken breasts, cut into pieces or strips

2 teaspoons hot pepper sauce

Juice of ½ lemon

Juice of ½ lime

1 green or red bell pepper, chopped

1 onion, chopped

2 cups chopped mushrooms

3 cups chopped broccoli

2 teaspoons lemon-pepper seasoning

2 cups hot cooked rice

✦ Heat the oil in a stir-fry pan over medium heat. Add the chicken, 1 teaspoon of the pepper sauce, 1 teaspoon of the lemon juice and 1 teaspoon of the lime juice; mix well.

✦ Reduce the heat to low. Cook for 25 to 30 minutes or until the chicken is cooked through. Drain and discard the pan drippings.

✦ Add the bell pepper, onion, mushrooms, broccoli, remaining pepper sauce, remaining lemon juice, remaining lime juice and lemon-pepper seasoning to the chicken mixture. Cook for 10 to 15 minutes or until the vegetables are tender-crisp.

✦ Serve over the rice.

✦ Yield: 6 servings

Gary Metivier
KWQC-TV6 Anchor

Coq au Vin

2 (7-pound) chickens
2 teaspoons salt
¼ teaspoon white pepper
¾ cup flour
½ cup olive oil
2 cups chopped onions
1½ cups chopped green bell peppers
2 cups quartered mushrooms
2 tablespoons chopped garlic
Bouquet garni (fresh parsley, bay leaf, dried thyme)
2 (28-ounce) cans crushed tomatoes
½ cup tomato juice
½ cup marsala or dry sherry

✦ Cut each chicken into 4 serving pieces. Combine the salt, white pepper and flour in a plastic bag; mix well. Add 2 to 3 pieces of chicken at a time and shake to coat with flour. Continue until all the chicken is coated.

✦ Heat the olive oil in a large skillet over medium-high heat. Add the chicken a few pieces at a time. Cook until brown on all sides. Remove the chicken to a large ovenproof sauté pan or lidded baking pan.

✦ Preheat the oven to 350 degrees. Add the onions, bell peppers, mushrooms and garlic to the skillet. Cook until the onions are soft, stirring occasionally. Spoon over the chicken.

✦ Tie the bouquet garni in cheesecloth and bury among the chicken pieces. Combine the tomatoes, tomato juice and marsala in a bowl; mix well. Spoon over the chicken. Bring to a boil over medium-high heat. Place in the oven.

✦ Bake, covered, for 35 minutes or until the chicken is cooked through. Discard the bouquet garni. Serve immediately.

✦ Yield: 8 servings

Louanne Walters
Former KWQC-TV6 Anchor

Sesame Chicken with Cumberland Sauce

2 (2½- to 3-pound) chickens

½ cup grated Parmesan cheese

2 cups seasoned bread crumbs

3 tablespoons sesame seeds

1 cup butter or margarine

1 cup currant jelly

1 (6-ounce) can frozen orange juice concentrate, thawed

½ cup dry sherry

1 teaspoon dry mustard

⅛ teaspoon ground ginger

¼ teaspoon hot pepper sauce

✦ Cut each chicken into serving pieces. Combine the cheese, bread crumbs and sesame seeds in a flat dish; mix well.

✦ Melt ¾ cup of the butter in a small skillet. Remove from the heat.

✦ Dip each chicken piece in the melted butter, then roll in the crumb mixture. Chill, covered, until ready to bake.

✦ Preheat the oven to 350 degrees. Place the chicken in a shallow 8x12-inch baking dish. Dot with the remaining ¼ cup butter. Bake for 1 hour or until the chicken is cooked through.

✦ For the sauce, combine the jelly, orange juice concentrate, sherry, mustard, ginger and hot pepper sauce in a saucepan; mix well.

✦ Cook over medium heat until the sauce is smooth, stirring occasionally. Serve with the chicken.

✦ Yield: 6 to 8 servings

Patricia Sundine-Edward
Former Host on WOC

Turkey Enchilada Casserole

1 pound ground turkey

1 teaspoon minced jalapeño, or to taste

1 teaspoon chopped green chiles, or to taste

2 tablespoons chopped onion

1 teaspoon minced garlic

12 small corn tortillas

2 (10-ounce) cans enchilada sauce

4 cups shredded Monterey Jack cheese

✦ Preheat the oven to 350 degrees. Brown the ground turkey in a skillet, stirring until crumbly; drain.

✦ Add the jalapeño, green chiles, onion and garlic. Cook until the onion is translucent, stirring occasionally.

✦ Dip a tortilla in the enchilada sauce in a shallow dish and place in the bottom of a 1½-quart casserole. Alternate layers of the ground turkey mixture, cheese and tortillas dipped in enchilada sauce in the casserole until all ingredients are used, ending with cheese and remaining enchilada sauce.

✦ Bake for 25 minutes. Garnish with sour cream and black olives.

✦ Yield: 4 to 6 servings

Carol LeBeau
Former WOC Anchor

Salmon Croquettes

3 tablespoons butter
¼ cup chopped onion
3 tablespoons flour
1 cup milk
1 cup cooked rice
1 (7-ounce) can salmon
1 cup cornflake crumbs
1 egg, beaten
1 cup shredded Cheddar cheese
1 to 2 cups cornflake crumbs for rolling

✦ Melt the butter in a saucepan over medium heat. Sauté the onion in the butter until translucent.

✦ Add the flour. Cook for 1 minute, stirring constantly. Whisk in the milk. Cook until thickened, stirring constantly.

✦ Transfer the cooked mixture to a large bowl. Add the rice, salmon, 1 cup cornflake crumbs, egg and cheese; mix well. Chill, covered, for 1 hour.

✦ Preheat the oven to 400 degrees. Coat a baking sheet with nonstick cooking spray.

✦ Shape the salmon mixture into patties. Roll in 1 to 2 cups cornflake crumbs to coat. Arrange the patties on the prepared baking sheet.

✦ Spray the tops of the patties with nonstick cooking spray. Bake for 20 minutes.

✦ Yield: 6 to 8 servings

Mexican Shrimp

2 tablespoons butter
½ cup chopped onion
⅓ cup chopped red or green bell pepper
2 jalapeños, chopped
1 tomato, chopped
1 (8-ounce) can tomato sauce
1 pound shrimp, peeled, deveined
2 cups hot cooked rice

✦ Melt the butter in a skillet over medium heat. Add the onion, bell pepper and jalapeños. Cook for 5 minutes or until tender.

✦ Add the tomato and tomato sauce. Bring to a boil. Add the shrimp. Reduce the heat.

✦ Simmer for 3 minutes or until the shrimp are pink and cooked through. Serve over the rice.

✦ Yield: 2 to 4 servings

DESSERTS

Thom Cornelis

Paula Sands

Gary Metivier

Terry Swails

KWQC-TV6

Community events and projects have always been an important part of KWQC-TV6. Events such as the annual Duck Race benefiting the Friendly House are a great way to have some fun and raise money.

KWQC-TV6

The American Cancer Society's annual Relay For Life, Christmas Walk, and Daffodil Days are just some of the events that generous KWQC-TV6 viewers have helped support throughout the years. In addition, the American Cancer Society operates two Discovery Shops in the Quad Cities.

Desserts

Angel Food Cake

1 cup sifted flour
1½ cups egg whites
¼ teaspoon salt
1 teaspoon cream of tartar
1 teaspoon vanilla extract
1½ cups sugar

✦ Preheat the oven to 325 degrees. Sift the flour 4 times; set aside. Beat the egg whites at low speed in a mixer bowl until foamy. Add the salt, cream of tartar and vanilla. Beat at medium speed until soft peaks form. Add the sugar 1 tablespoon at a time, beating constantly at high speed until stiff peaks form. Fold in the flour gently ¼ cup at a time.

✦ Spoon into an ungreased tube pan and smooth the top. Bake for 1¼ hours or until the top is brown and dry.

✦ Remove the cake from the oven and immediately invert on a funnel to cool completely.

✦ Yield: 16 servings

Mrs. Richard Petty
Wife of Race Car Driver Richard Petty

When WOC signed on the air in 1949, it utilized programming from four sources: local live programs from the WOC studios; network programs by kinescope recordings (sent by air express to TV stations that were not yet on the connected network); motion picture films; and local live remote programs outside the studio.

Red Devil's Food Cake

1½ cups sugar
½ cup shortening
½ cup baking cocoa
2 eggs, beaten
1 teaspoon vanilla extract
½ cup milk or buttermilk
1 cup cold water
2 teaspoons baking soda
2 cups flour

✦ Preheat the oven to 375 degrees. Grease and flour a 9x10-inch cake pan. Cream the sugar and shortening in a mixer bowl until light and fluffy. Add the baking cocoa, eggs and vanilla; beat until smooth. Add the milk and water; beat until smooth.

✦ Combine the baking soda and flour in a bowl; mix well. Add to the creamed mixture gradually, beating constantly until smooth.

✦ Pour the batter into the prepared cake pan. Bake for 40 minutes or until the cake tests done.

✦ Yield: 12 to 15 servings

My Favorite Chocolate Cake

½ cup baking cocoa
½ cup hot water
½ cup margarine, softened
1½ cups sugar
1 cup buttermilk
1 teaspoon vanilla extract
2 eggs, beaten
2 cups flour
1 teaspoon baking soda

✦ Preheat the oven to 350 degrees. Grease and flour a 9x13-inch cake pan.

✦ Heat the baking cocoa and hot water in a saucepan over medium-high heat, stirring frequently until the mixture is smooth. Set aside to cool.

✦ Cream the margarine and sugar in a mixer bowl until light and fluffy. Add the cooled baking cocoa mixture; mix well. Add the buttermilk, vanilla and eggs; mix until smooth.

✦ Sift the flour and baking soda together. Add to the batter and beat until smooth.

✦ Pour into the prepared cake pan. Bake for 35 to 40 minutes or until the cake tests done.

✦ Yield: 15 to 18 servings

Jennifer Mooney
Wife of former KWQC-TV6 Anchor John Mooney

Marie's Pineapple Cake

1½ cups butter, softened

2 cups sugar

6 eggs

4 teaspoons lemon extract

1 tablespoon vanilla extract

2 cups milk

3 cups self-rising flour, sifted

2 (8-ounce) cans crushed pineapple, drained

2 cups confectioners' sugar

1 (14-ounce) package coconut

✦ Preheat the oven to 350 degrees. Grease and flour two 9-inch cake pans.

✦ Cream the butter and sugar in a mixer bowl until light and fluffy. Add the eggs 1 at a time, mixing well after each addition. Add the lemon extract, vanilla and milk; mix well. Add the flour gradually, mixing constantly until smooth.

✦ Pour into the prepared cake pans. Bake for 25 to 30 minutes or until the layers test done. Remove from the oven and cool completely.

✦ For the frosting, combine the pineapple and confectioners' sugar in a bowl; mix well. Stir in half the coconut.

✦ Spread the frosting between the layers and over the top and side of the cooled cake. Sprinkle the remaining coconut over the top.

✦ Yield: 12 servings

Strawberry Special

1 (2-layer) package white cake mix

1 (3-ounce) package strawberry gelatin

3/4 cup vegetable oil

4 eggs

1/4 cup water

1 (16-ounce) package frozen sliced strawberries, thawed

2 cups confectioners' sugar

Whipped topping (optional)

✦ Preheat the oven to 350 degrees. Grease and flour a 9x13-inch cake pan.

✦ Combine the cake mix and gelatin in a bowl. Add the oil, eggs, water and half the strawberries; mix well.

✦ Pour the batter into the prepared cake pan. Bake for 35 to 40 minutes or until the cake tests done. Remove from the oven and poke holes evenly over the top of the cake with a fork or toothpick.

✦ Mix the confectioners' sugar and remaining strawberries in a bowl, stirring until the confectioners' sugar is dissolved.

✦ Pour the strawberry mixture over the top of the cake. Serve immediately with whipped topping.

✦ Yield: 12 to 15 servings

Watergate Cake

1 (2-layer) package white cake mix

1 (4-ounce) package pistachio instant pudding mix

1 cup club soda

1 cup vegetable oil

3 eggs

16 ounces whipped topping

1 (4-ounce) package pistachio instant pudding mix

1 can chocolate syrup

✦ Preheat the oven to 350 degrees. Grease and flour a 9x12-inch cake pan.

✦ For the cake, combine the cake mix, 1 package pudding mix, club soda, oil and eggs in a mixer bowl. Beat at high speed for 4 minutes or until smooth and creamy. Pour the batter into the prepared cake pan.

✦ Bake for 35 minutes or until cake tests done. Remove from the oven and cool in the pan for 10 minutes. Remove to a wire rack to cool completely.

✦ For the frosting, mix the whipped topping and 1 package pudding mix in a bowl until smooth. Spread over the top of the cake.

✦ Drizzle the chocolate syrup over the frosting in a decorative pattern.

✦ Yield: 15 to 18 servings

Christmas Fudge

4½ cups sugar

½ cup butter

1 (12-ounce) can evaporated milk

1 teaspoon salt

2 cups semisweet chocolate chips

1 (7-ounce) jar marshmallow creme

2 teaspoons vanilla extract

2 cups chopped pecans

✦ Combine the sugar, butter, evaporated milk and salt in a saucepan. Cook over medium-high heat until the mixture begins to boil, stirring constantly. Cook for 7 minutes, stirring constantly.

✦ Remove from the heat and add the chocolate chips and marshmallow creme. Beat with an electric mixer at medium speed for 3 minutes or until well blended.

✦ Stir in the vanilla and pecans.

✦ Pour the mixture into a buttered pan. Cool completely before cutting.

✦ Yield: 5 pounds

Mike Mickle
KWQC-TV6 Anchor

Favorite Fudge

4 cups sugar

1 teaspoon vanilla extract

1 cup butter

1 cup milk

25 large marshmallows, cut into quarters

2 cups semisweet chocolate chips

2 cups milk chocolate chips

2 ounces unsweetened chocolate

1 cup chopped pecans or walnuts

✦ Combine the sugar, vanilla, butter and milk in a saucepan. Boil over medium-high heat for 2 minutes, stirring constantly. Remove from the heat.

✦ Add the marshmallows, stirring until melted. Add the semisweet chocolate chips; stir until melted. Add the milk chocolate chips; stir until melted. Add the unsweetened chocolate; stir until melted. Stir in the pecans.

✦ Pour into a greased 11x15-inch pan. Cool until firm before cutting.

✦ Yield: 5 pounds

Chocolate Peanut Blossom Cookies

1¾ cups flour
1 teaspoon baking soda
½ teaspoon salt
½ cup sugar
½ cup packed brown sugar
½ cup shortening
1 teaspoon vanilla extract
1 egg, beaten
2 tablespoons milk
½ cup peanut butter
Sugar for coating
48 chocolate kisses

✦ Preheat the oven to 350 degrees. Combine the flour, baking soda and salt in a bowl; mix well.

✦ Cream ½ cup sugar, brown sugar, shortening and vanilla in a mixer bowl until light and fluffy. Add the egg and milk; mix well. Add the peanut butter. Beat at low speed until the dough forms a ball and leaves the side of the bowl.

✦ Shape the dough into 1-inch balls. Roll the balls in additional sugar and place on an ungreased cookie sheet.

✦ Bake for 10 to 12 minutes or until lightly browned. Remove from the oven and place a chocolate kiss in the center of each cookie. Press down firmly until the cookie cracks around the edge.

✦ Cool for 2 minutes on the cookie sheet. Remove to a wire rack to cool completely.

✦ Yield: 4 dozen

Chocolate Malted Cookies

1 cup butter-flavored shortening

1¼ cups packed brown sugar

½ cup malted milk powder

2 tablespoons chocolate syrup

1 tablespoon vanilla extract

1 egg, beaten

2 cups flour

1 teaspoon baking soda

½ teaspoon salt

1½ cups semisweet chocolate chunks

1 cup milk chocolate chips

✦ Preheat the oven to 375 degrees. Combine the shortening, brown sugar, milk powder, chocolate syrup and vanilla in a mixer bowl. Beat at high speed for 2 minutes. Add the egg; beat well.

✦ Combine the flour, baking soda and salt in a bowl; mix well. Add to the creamed mixture gradually, mixing well after each addition. Stir in the chocolate chunks and milk chocolate chips.

✦ Shape the dough into 2-inch balls. Place 3 inches apart on an ungreased cookie sheet.

✦ Bake for 12 to 14 minutes or until golden brown. Cool for 5 minutes on the cookie sheet. Remove to a wire rack to cool completely.

✦ Yield: 1½ dozen

Lace Cookies

½ cup flour
½ cup shredded coconut
¼ cup corn syrup
¼ cup packed brown sugar
¼ cup margarine, softened
½ teaspoon vanilla extract

✦ Preheat the oven to 325 degrees. Combine the flour and coconut in a mixer bowl.

✦ Combine the corn syrup, brown sugar and margarine in a saucepan. Cook over medium heat until the mixture is melted, stirring constantly. Remove from the heat and stir in the vanilla.

✦ Add the flour mixture gradually to the brown sugar mixture, mixing well after each addition.

✦ Drop by rounded teaspoonfuls 3 inches apart onto an ungreased cookie sheet. Bake for 6 to 8 minutes or until golden brown. Remove to a wire rack to cool.

✦ Yield: 1 dozen

Mrs. Lyndon Johnson
Widow of President Lyndon Johnson

Old-Fashioned Molasses Cookies

1 cup shortening
1½ cups unsulphured molasses
¼ cup sugar
4 cups sifted flour
1½ teaspoons salt
2 teaspoons baking soda
2 teaspoons ground cinnamon
1½ teaspoons ground ginger
½ teaspoon ground cloves
1 egg, beaten

✦ Melt the shortening in a large saucepan over medium heat. Add the molasses and sugar; mix well. Remove from the heat; set aside.

✦ Sift the flour, salt, baking soda, cinnamon, ginger and cloves together in a bowl. Stir ¼ cup of the flour mixture into the molasses mixture. Add the egg; mix well. Add the remaining flour mixture. Beat until smooth. Chill the dough for 2 hours.

✦ Preheat the oven to 350 degrees. Shape the dough into ¼-inch balls.

✦ Place the balls 1 inch apart on ungreased cookie sheets. Bake for 15 minutes.

✦ Remove to a wire rack to cool. Store in an airtight container.

✦ Yield: 5 dozen

Charles King
KWQC-TV6 Anchor

Peppernuts

1½ cups packed brown sugar

1 cup margarine, softened

1 egg, beaten

2 teaspoons ground cinnamon

¼ teaspoon ground ginger

⅛ teaspoon ground cloves

Pinch of pepper

1 tablespoon molasses

3 cups flour

✦ Cream the brown sugar, margarine and egg in a mixer bowl until light and fluffy. Add the cinnamon, ginger, cloves, pepper and molasses; mix well. Add the flour gradually, mixing well after each addition. Chill the dough for 20 minutes.

✦ Preheat the oven to 350 degrees. Roll the dough into finger-size logs. Cut each into ½-inch pieces and arrange on a nonstick cookie sheet.

✦ Bake for 10 minutes. Remove to a wire rack to cool.

✦ Yield: 2 dozen

John Mooney hands the baton to Gary Metivier in the spring of 1998.

Snickerdoodles

½ cup margarine or butter, softened

½ cup shortening

1½ cups sugar

2 medium eggs, beaten

2¾ cups flour

2 teaspoons cream of tartar

1 teaspoon baking soda

¼ teaspoon salt

2 tablespoons sugar

2 teaspoons ground cinnamon

✦ Cream the margarine, shortening, 1½ cups sugar and eggs in a mixer bowl until light and fluffy.

✦ Combine the flour, cream of tartar, baking soda and salt in a bowl; mix well. Add to the creamed mixture gradually, mixing well after each addition. Chill the dough for 2 to 3 hours.

✦ Preheat the oven to 400 degrees. Combine 2 tablespoons sugar and cinnamon in a shallow bowl. Shape the dough by rounded teaspoonfuls into balls. Roll in the cinnamon sugar.

✦ Place the balls 2 inches apart on an ungreased cookie sheet. Bake for 8 to 10 minutes. Remove immediately to a wire rack to cool.

✦ Yield: 4 to 5 dozen

Delicious Sugar Cookies

1 cup margarine, softened
1 cup shortening
1 cup sugar
1 cup confectioners' sugar
2 eggs, beaten
2 teaspoons vanilla extract
4 cups flour
1 teaspoon baking soda
1 teaspoon cream of tartar
Sugar for coating

✦ Cream the margarine, shortening and 1 cup sugar in a mixer bowl until light and fluffy. Add the confectioners' sugar, eggs and vanilla. Beat until smooth.

✦ Sift the flour, baking soda and cream of tartar together in a bowl. Add to the creamed mixture gradually, mixing well after each addition until a smooth dough forms. Chill for 1 hour.

✦ Preheat the oven to 350 degrees. Shape the dough by teaspoonfuls into balls and roll in additional sugar.

✦ Place the balls 2 inches apart on a nonstick cookie sheet. Flatten with the bottom of a glass. Bake for 20 minutes or until brown around the edges. Remove to a wire rack to cool.

✦ Yield: 4 dozen

Thumbprint Cookies

1 cup shortening
1 cup margarine, softened
1 cup packed brown sugar
4 egg yolks
2 teaspoons vanilla extract
1 teaspoon salt
4 cups sifted flour
4 egg whites
3 cups finely chopped pecans or walnuts
Butter cream frosting (optional)

✦ Preheat the oven to 375 degrees. Cream the shortening, margarine, brown sugar, egg yolks, vanilla and salt in a mixer bowl until light and fluffy. Add the flour gradually, mixing well after each addition.

✦ Beat the egg whites lightly in a shallow bowl until foamy. Place the pecans in a bowl. Shape the dough by rounded teaspoonfuls into balls. Roll in the egg whites, then in the pecans. Place 2 inches apart on a nonstick cookie sheet.

✦ Bake for 5 minutes. Remove from the oven and press the center of each cookie with your thumb. Return the cookies to the oven.

✦ Bake for 8 minutes. Remove from the oven. Fill the thumbprints with butter cream frosting. Remove to a wire rack to cool.

✦ Yield: 4 dozen

Swedish Farmer Cookies

1 cup butter, softened
¾ cup sugar
1 tablespoon dark corn syrup
⅓ cup chopped blanched almonds
2 cups flour
1 teaspoon baking soda
Pinch of salt

✦ Cream the butter and sugar in a mixer bowl until light and fluffy. Add the corn syrup and almonds; mix well.

✦ Sift the flour, baking soda and salt together in a bowl. Sift the flour mixture into the creamed mixture; mix well.

✦ Shape the dough into logs. Wrap in waxed paper. Chill for 2 hours.

✦ Preheat the oven to 350 degrees. Slice the dough logs thinly. Place the rounds on a greased cookie sheet. Bake for 8 to 10 minutes or until golden brown. Remove to a wire rack to cool.

✦ Yield: 2 dozen

Sharon DeRycke
KWQC-TV6 Anchor

Fudge Pecan Pie

½ cup sugar
1¼ cups light corn syrup
3 eggs
3 tablespoons melted butter
1½ teaspoons vanilla extract
⅓ cup baking cocoa
⅓ cup flour
¼ teaspoon salt
½ cup chopped pecans
1 unbaked (9-inch) pie shell
½ cup pecan halves

✦ Preheat the oven to 350 degrees. Cream the sugar, corn syrup, eggs, butter and vanilla in a mixer bowl until light and fluffy. Add the baking cocoa, flour and salt. Beat for 30 seconds at medium speed. Stir in the chopped pecans.

✦ Spoon into the pie shell. Arrange the pecan halves over the top.

✦ Bake for 1 hour. Cool completely before serving.

✦ Yield: 6 to 8 servings

Paula Sands
KWQC-TV6 Anchor and Host of
"Paula Sands Live"

Mama Vesey's Sweet Potato Pie

4 to 5 sweet potatoes, boiled, peeled

1 cup butter, softened

3 eggs, beaten

3 cups (or more) sugar

¼ cup evaporated milk

1 tablespoon flour

1 tablespoon lemon extract, or to taste

2 teaspoons vanilla extract

1 unbaked (9-inch) pie shell

✦ Preheat the oven to 350 degrees. Beat the sweet potatoes, butter, eggs and sugar in a mixer bowl at medium speed until smooth. Add the evaporated milk, flour, lemon extract and vanilla. Beat until smooth.

✦ Pour into the pie shell. Bake for 45 minutes or until the filling is set and the edge of the pie shell is golden brown.

✦ Yield: 6 to 8 servings

Easy-as-Pie Cheesecake

2½ cups graham cracker crumbs

¼ cup sugar

½ cup melted butter

24 ounces cream cheese, softened

4 eggs

1 cup sugar

1 teaspoon vanilla extract

1 cup sour cream

2 tablespoons sugar

1 teaspoon vanilla extract

✦ Preheat the oven to 350 degrees. For the crust, combine the cracker crumbs, ¼ cup sugar and butter in a bowl; mix well. Press into a 9x13-inch baking pan.

✦ For the filling, beat the cream cheese, eggs and 1 cup sugar in a mixer bowl until light and fluffy. Add 1 teaspoon vanilla; mix well. Pour into the prepared crust.

✦ Bake for 30 minutes. Cool completely.

✦ For the topping, mix the sour cream, 2 tablespoons sugar and 1 teaspoon vanilla in a bowl until creamy. Spread over the top of the cooled cheesecake.

✦ Yield: 20 servings

Jason DeRusha
KWQC-TV6 Anchor

Cherry Cheesecake Cups

12 vanilla wafers

16 ounces light cream cheese, softened

2 eggs

2 teaspoons vanilla extract

½ cup sugar

1 (21-ounce) can reduced-calorie cherry pie filling

✦ Preheat the oven to 375 degrees. Line 12 muffin cups with paper liners. Place 1 vanilla wafer in the bottom of each.

✦ Beat the cream cheese, eggs, vanilla and sugar in a mixer bowl for 5 minutes at medium speed. Pour into the prepared muffin cups.

✦ Bake for 10 to 15 minutes or until the tops crack slightly.

✦ Cool completely. Top each cheesecake cup with a spoonful of the pie filling. Chill until serving time.

✦ Yield: 12 servings

Rich Chocolate Cups

8 ounces cream cheese, softened

1/3 cup sugar

1/8 teaspoon salt

1 egg

1/2 cup miniature semisweet chocolate chips

1 1/4 cups flour

1 cup sugar

1/3 cup baking cocoa

3/4 teaspoon baking soda

1/2 teaspoon salt

1 cup buttermilk

1/3 cup vegetable oil

1 egg, beaten

1 teaspoon vanilla extract

✦ Preheat the oven to 350 degrees. For the filling, beat the cream cheese, 1/3 cup sugar, 1/8 teaspoon salt and 1 egg in a mixer bowl until light and fluffy. Stir in the chocolate chips. Set aside.

✦ For the cupcakes, combine the flour, 1 cup sugar, baking cocoa, baking soda and 1/2 teaspoon salt in a mixer bowl; mix well. Add the buttermilk, oil, 1 egg and vanilla; mix well.

✦ Pour the batter into 24 paper-lined muffin cups, filling each half full. Spoon 1 tablespoon of the filling over the center of each cupcake. Bake for 30 minutes or until the tops are golden brown.

✦ Yield: 24 servings

Paula Sands
KWQC-TV6 Anchor and Host of
"Paula Sands Live"

After-Hours Tiramisù

1 pound mascarpone cheese, softened

1 cup sugar

1 egg, beaten

1 tablespoon vanilla extract

6 tablespoons almond liqueur

2 cups whipping cream, whipped

5 cups espresso, chilled

40 ladyfingers

1 cup grated semisweet chocolate

✦ Cream the mascarpone cheese and sugar in a mixer bowl until light and fluffy. Add the egg, vanilla and 2 tablespoons of the liqueur; mix well. Fold in the whipped cream gently.

✦ Combine the espresso and remaining liqueur in a bowl; mix well.

✦ Spread a layer of the whipped cream mixture 1/4 inch thick and 5 inches wide down the center of a 9x16-inch baking sheet. Dip the ladyfingers into the espresso mixture lightly. Arrange 1 layer of the ladyfingers over the whipped cream mixture.

✦ Spread a 1/2-inch layer of the whipped cream mixture over the ladyfingers. Sprinkle with 1/4 of the chocolate.

✦ Repeat the layers twice, ending with the chocolate. Arrange the ladyfinger layers in different directions for sturdiness. Chill for 40 minutes or until firm.

✦ Yield: 12 servings

Beth Perry
KWQC-TV6 Reporter

Rhubarb Crunch

4 cups chopped rhubarb
1⅓ cups sugar
1¼ cups flour
¾ cup sugar
½ teaspoon salt
½ cup margarine

✦ Preheat the oven to 350 degrees. Place the rhubarb in the bottom of a buttered casserole. Sprinkle with 1⅓ cups sugar; toss to mix well.

✦ Combine the flour, ¾ cup sugar and salt in a bowl; mix well. Sprinkle over the rhubarb.

✦ Dot with the margarine. Bake for 30 to 45 minutes or until bubbly.

✦ Yield: 8 servings

Heavenly Hash

8 ounces milk chocolate

1 (14-ounce) can sweetened condensed milk

2 (10-ounce) packages miniature marshmallows

1 cup chopped pecans or walnuts

✦ Combine the chocolate with 1 to 2 tablespoons of the condensed milk in the top of a double boiler. Cook until the chocolate is melted, stirring frequently. Stir in the remaining condensed milk.

✦ Combine the marshmallows and pecans in a buttered 9x9-inch dish; mix well. Pour the chocolate mixture over the pecans and marshmallows. Cool completely before cutting.

✦ Yield: 2 pounds

Butter Brickle Ice Cream Dessert

12 saltine crackers

12 graham crackers

½ cup melted margarine

2 cups milk

2 (4-ounce) packages French vanilla instant pudding mix

1 quart butter brickle ice cream, softened

Whipped topping

2 Heath candy bars, crushed

✦ Process the saltines and graham crackers in a food processor until fine crumbs form. Transfer the crumbs to a bowl.

✦ Add the margarine; mix well. Press the mixture into a 9x13-inch glass dish.

✦ Beat the milk and pudding mix in a mixer bowl for 1 minute at medium speed. Add the ice cream. Beat for 1 minute or until blended. Pour into the prepared dish. Chill until set.

✦ Spread whipped topping over the ice cream mixture. Sprinkle with the candy.

✦ Yield: 24 servings

Fran Riley
KWQC-TV6 Anchor

Index

KWQC-TV6

50th Anniversary Cookbook

A Collection of Recipes & Memories

Please send me ______ copies of the *50th Anniversary Cookbook* @ $17.95 per book $_________

Postage and Handling at $3.50 per book $_________

Total $_________

Name

Address

City State Zip

Phone Number

Method of Payment: [ ] VISA [ ] MasterCard

[ ] Check payable to KWQC-TV6 Cookbook

Account Number Expiration Date

Cardholder Name

Signature

To order by mail, send to: KWQC-TV6 Cookbook
P.O. Box 4545 • Davenport, Iowa 52808-4545 • (319) 383-7000

Photocopies accepted.